THE NEW RESPONSE:

Contemporary Painters of the Hudson River

Albany Institute of History and Art
125 Washington Avenue, Albany, N.Y. 12210
November 8, 1985 - January 15, 1986

Vassar College Art Gallery
Vassar College, Poughkeepsie, N.Y. 12601
January 27 - March 23, 1986

Artists' Choice Museum
394 West Broadway, New York, N.Y. 10012
April 19 - May 18, 1986

THE NEW RESPONSE:
Contemporary Painters of the Hudson River

Exhibition organized by Thomas Nelson

Co-curated by John Yau and Thomas Nelson

Catalogue by John Yau

Introduction by Alan Gussow

ALBANY INSTITUTE OF HISTORY AND ART

Cover Illustration:
Palisades
by Bill Sullivan
oil on canvas, 1984
48 x 78 inches

This catalogue has been made possible by a
generous grant from the American
Express Foundation

Photographic credits:
no. 1 Dorothy Zeidman
nos. 3, 10 Earl Ripling
nos. 8, 11, 14a & b, 24 Lou Carol Lecce
no. 4 Adam Reich
no. 7b Ralph Gabriner
no. 15 Radio Photo
no. 19 Elton Pope-Lance
no. 25 Ken Cohen
Other photographs courtesy of the lenders

Published by The Albany Institute of History and Art
Library of Congress catalogue number 85-73133
ISBN 0-939072-05-X
©Copyright 1985 by Scenic Hudson Inc.
Designed by Thomas Nelson
Printed by Lane Press, Albany, N.Y.

This Catalogue and Exhibition are a tribute to a new generation of Hudson River Artists.

Table of Contents

The exhibition is sponsored by Scenic Hudson Inc., with the
assistance of the American Express Foundation.

Acknowledgments

Many people and organizations contributed their help and support toward the realization of this exhibition and publication. I would first like to thank the staff of the Albany Institute of History and Art, especially Joseph Reeves, Director of Publications, and Christine Robinson, Registrar. Norman Rice and Roderic Blackburn, Director and Assistant Director of the Albany Institute, provided advice that eased the months of preparatory work. I would also like to thank Jan Ernst Adlmann, Director of the Vassar College Art Gallery, and his assistant, Donice English, for adding this exhibition to their schedule, and insuring a wider audience.

Scenic Hudson Inc. has forged many links with artists, their works, and the environment. I am indebted to this organization, especially Frances Reese, Chairman Emeritus, and Florence Penella, Director of Planning, for their support and fund raising endeavors, making possible this fitting new tribute to the River and its environs. I hope that this exhibition has contributed in some small way to the efforts of those interested in preserving such a vital resource as the Hudson River—a task that Scenic Hudson has admirably undertaken for some twenty years.

I deeply appreciate the interest and cooperation of the numerous galleries, museums, corporations, and individuals for their generosity in loaning paintings for the exhibition and photographs for use in the catalogue (a complete list of lenders appears on page 80.)

Alan Gussow's thoughtful essay on the aesthetic legacy of the Hudson River Valley enables us to appreciate more fully the implications of this body of work as both a continuation of and reaction to the work of the nineteenth century Hudson River School painters. A long-time resident of the Hudson Valley, Gussow is an accomplished artist, author, teacher, lecturer and environmental consultant. His book and exhibition *A Sense of Place, The Artist and the American Land* were influential in the conception and format of this exhibition.

It has been a pleasure to work with John Yau, whose knowledge and insights on contemporary art were indispensable to this project. Despite his busy schedule, John has provided a detailed and perceptive summary of the artists represented in this exhibition. I thank John and hope that we will have the opportunity to collaborate on future exhibitions.

TN

This exhibition, one of the Albany Institute of Hisory and Art's most significant exhibitions of contemporary art, is the result of almost two years of sifting through slides, letters and catalogues as well as visiting galleries and studios. The result is a visual delight. The stylistic range of the work included encompasses almost as many modes as there exist in contemporary painting. The whole is unified by one common element—all of these works are related to the Hudson River Valley area from New York City to the Adirondacks. In looking over these works one cannot help but be struck by both the familiarity of the scenes and the various manners in which the artists have chosen to respond to them.

An artist does not change his or her approach to a subject simply because of its geographic location. Most of the artists in this exhibition cannot be called exclusively painters of the Hudson Valley region. Many paint and have painted other subjects. What makes this exhibition unique is that by bringing together these thirty-six paintings, by almost as many artists, one becomes aware of the diversity as well as the recurring elements that seem to be one of the hallmarks of American art of the past half-decade.

It seems apropos that a museum with an important collection of nineteenth century Hudson River School paintings should undertake a look at what contemporary painters are doing with the same region.

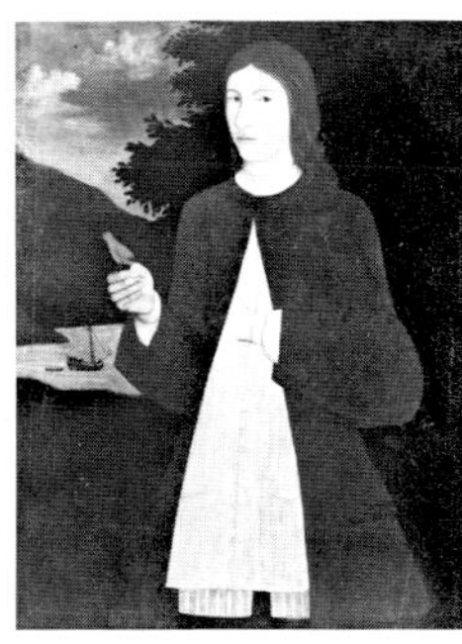

Pieter Vanderlyn (1687-1778)
Pau de Wanderlaer, ca. 1730
Oil on canvas, 44½ x 35 inches
Collection of the Albany Institute of History and Art

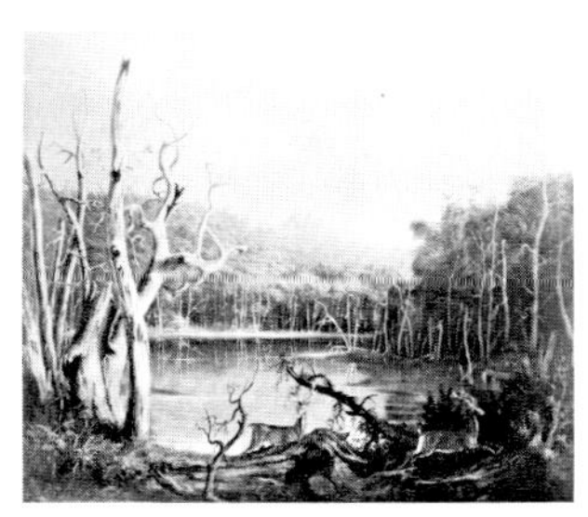

Thomas Cole (1801-1848)
Lake with Dead Trees (Catskills), 1825
Oil on canvas, 27 x 34 inches
Courtesy of the Allen Memorial Art Museum
Oberlin College, Oberlin, Ohio

Actually, the first depiction of a Hudson River scene in an American painting appears in an eighteenth century limner portrait, *Pau de Wandelaer*, c. 1730, by Pieter Vanderlyn (1687-1778). From this rather humble beginning, the romantic, nature-inspired Hudson River School commenced nearly one hundred years later. Not surprisingly, artists have found that to the present day, the Hudson River remains a viable source of inspiration.

This exhibition is not meant to exemplify a new "Hudson River School" — it is intended to be much broader. It was my original intention to illustrate the various modes or "responses" that contemporary painters have toward the region that has influenced artists for more than two centuries. There may be several artists whose works merit inclusion whom we may have inadvertently neglected, yet my co-curator John Yau and I feel that the exhibition we have assembled is comprehensive and to the point of its intention. This exhibition brings together for the first time a group of work that, to the best of our knowledge, represents the most important painting being done concerning the idea of this "New Response" — that is, a new view of nature and of a particular geographic locale so important to the history of the American art.

Thomas E. Nelson
Curator of Exhibitions

Introduction

A LAND WE KNOW BUT HAVE NOT VALUED —
Visions of New Beauty in the Hudson River Valley
Alan Gussow

Since the early 1800s when Thomas Cole first ventured into the Kaaterskill Clove, the Hudson River Valley has retained a special, perhaps unique, attraction for working artists. Modest in scale (the Catskills cannot be confused with the Rockies), rich in texture and forms, laden with historic associations, maintained by the love and care of its residents, and pulled together by the flowing ribbon which is the Hudson River itself, this fortunate region has prompted generations of artists to return again and again for inspiration.

Why the "Hudson River School" of landscape painting? Why the Hudson River as a special place? What is it about this valley — no longer virginal, no longer pristine, barely if at all wild—that it continues to attract working artists?

The possibility of direct encounter with nature was no doubt the original appeal of the Hudson River Valley, "nature that was new to art," as Thomas Cole once wrote. Here was an uncorrupted rural area, a place that could be portrayed "without investing it with heroes, myths and legends," as Jo Miller notes. Yet by a curious and ironic twist, the artists who were drawn to the Hudson River Valley because it was new, undiscovered, unportrayed, without cultural overtones, and who painted the grottoes, waterfalls, shoreline, and vistas with an unprecedented freshness of discovery, were the same artists who attached a lingering value to the region merely by responding to the place.

The work of the earliest Hudson River painters is characterized by a narrative based wholly on experience, on seeing for oneself. The result of their effort was not so much to create a "school" of painting as it was to develop and promote an attitude toward subject matter. "Go first to nature" was Asher Durand's advice, and so they did. The emphasis was as much on the "going" as it was on "nature." One of the favorite base camps of the nineteenth century was the small, primitive village of Palenville at the foot of the Kaaterskill Clove, a place which contemporary letters describe in terms of "wet-floored bars, close room(ed) unpleasantness...(and) lawlessness." Being in Palenville created a sense of anticipation, of shared adventure, of camaraderie. Painting was rugged business then, and the search for vista points and moist grottoes was physically demanding. The Hudson River artists declared a dual independence—first, from the cultured traditions of Europe, and second, as pioneers in a search for rural beauty.

There, perhaps, lies the key to the continued allure of the Valley as a mecca for artists. The painting tradition of the region was shaped more by nature than by art. The result is that artists—even contemporary artists—are bound less by approved styles of painting than by the molding influence of the natural forms in the Valley itself. An artist going out to work in the Hudson River Valley today is accompanied by the spiritual presence of Cole, Church, Durand, and their nineteenth century brotherhood, but she or he is not arbitrarily framed by nineteenth century conventions. Nature is still there to be responded to, in new ways with new forms.

Obviously, appearances have changed. The shoreline is often blighted. Billboards and transmission lines mar the scenic beauty. Automobile graveyards compete with historic homes for dominance in the visual field. Yet the Hudson River is still there, its scale in places surprisingly large, and the cloves, waterfalls, grottoes and reaches remain. Where the natural setting has suffered, the tradition of the nineteenth century softens the blow. It is not Cole's art or Durand's which is likely to influence a young artist today; it is the fact that Cole and Durand and Kensett and Church trod the same paths, looked out from the same vista point and laid claim for all artists to this region.

So the early artists, choosing places which lacked heroes and myths, must have contributed to the creation of a landscape in which they have become mythographers themselves. A nature painter working in the Hudson River Valley today cannot ignore the fact that the surrounding hills possess a meaning given them by artists a century ago. This valley is no ordinary setting; it is a cultural landscape with a long, durable, potent art history. Such a tradition can be an ally, or it can be a force one must overcome.

"To become a figurative or realistic painter, above all, a landscape artist, in the nineteen fifties and sixties, took a lion kind of courage," poet L.E. Sissman once wrote. Somewhat less courage may be required in the nineteen eighties, which are more determinedly pluralistic. Yet every landscape painter experiences that solitary and often frightening moment when a choice of subject matter must be made. The fact that the gallery and museum world may embrace landscape painting more readily today than it did in the nineteen sixties does not make the act of painting from nature any easier. Artists who work from the land must still find a way to establish an intimate relationship with the environment, and they must decide for themselves what constitutes appropriate subject matter.

When Marjorie Portnow, an artist now resident in Hudson, was asked, "What makes you set up to work in a certain place?" she responded, "Because it looks like a painting!" We are left to speculate whether the places she chooses look like nineteenth century paintings or somehow conform to her own evolving aesthetic. Portnow's paintings are obviously the key to her answer.

Some artists of *The New Response* are clearly wedded to an earlier vision of the Hudson River Valley. George Wexler, a painter from New Paltz, speaks for the traditionalists. "Not long ago (he was speaking in 1972) I became very much aware of nineteenth century American painting. My whole background...has always oriented me to despise this work. As I got older, I started to look at things a little more freshly. The Hudson River School painters! That's where I live; they were working with the same things I'm working with. There's an affinity here which I now feel through nature." Marcia Clark, a painter from Rifton, was drawn to the valley more by the living landscape than by art history, saying simply, "I moved here because it was so beautiful and there were endless choices in subject matter. The excitement of being here was very abstract, yet it was here that I started to work from closer observation."

The contemporary painter in the Hudson River Valley extends a formidable tradition. Whether the past is perceived as a burden or an inspiration depends upon the individual artist. What appears critical for each painter is not the potential domination by nineteenth century traditions but rather the working out of a sustaining relationship with a particular landscape, a relationship which acknowledges earlier visions and yet is open to new experiences. The difficulty of reckoning with past traditions while allowing the necessary time to form productive relationships with the living landscape was much on Catherine Murphy's mind when she recently talked about her move to Hyde

Park. "I didn't want to move here because of the Hudson River School. Art and art history was a system of taking things apart, taking things to pieces. I became a realist because I don't want pieces, I want the whole. Jesus, I don't want a piece of it. I want everything. Realism for me was a combination of all the parts. The reason I am a realist at all," she continued, "is to connect with the world, not landscape specifically, but just connecting. When I sit down in a new environment, it takes me a long time. Mostly I have to find myself in that environment, to find my own vision. You've got to resist what you are seeing and (yet) in some ways relate to what you are seeing. You have to find that place where you belong in that idea. I was very frightened to move to the country. It was the first time I had to confront landscape without man-made geometry. (Most of all) we've got to go out and see nature again."

When artists move through the Hudson River Valley today, what sort of landscape do they find? What is it about this place that seduces their eyes? More to the point, to what qualities in the scene do contemporary painters respond? Thomas Cole often sought the sublime setting, one that would stir deep religious feelings. Today's painters talk of profound encounters with nature, yet the sites they select to depict are often more modest, less grandiose, more local and vernacular. Marjorie Portnow was lured to the Hudson River Valley because she found it an "interesting combination of civilized and rough," what Marcia Clark termed "the rough and the not-so-rough." Robert Berlind purchased a run-down farm on the edge of the Catskill mountains in Sullivan County—rolling, hummocking land. What he is attracted to is simply "something going on," events which he believes *undermine* rather than enhance the sublime. Alan Cote bought a tugboat repair shop in Kingston from which he can watch the river's changing activity. His pleasure comes when he rows out into the space which he has observed. These artists and others find satisfaction in deepening their awareness of the landscape that surrounds them. They feel little need to go off in search of scenery as did so many of the nineteenth century artists.

If Thomas Cole, Asher Durand, Frederic Church, and others of their period taught us to know what was beautiful in the landscape—and they did—then artists today are instructing us in another kind of beauty. The earlier painters glorified the glades, knolls, scenic vistas and spectacular waterfalls. In their paintings they unintentionally created visual models for generations of park and highway designers. Today's painters, residents of the valley, not tourists, are portraying a simpler, more modest beauty, a less aggressive landscape which incorporates human activity. There are exceptions, of course. Don Nice of Putnam County, made curious by "seeing the river pass by," decided to go to the Hudson's source at Lake Tear of the Clouds. I, myself, have returned to the Kaaterskill Clove in ritual acts of pilgrimage. Yet few artists in the valley today seek strenuous encounters with wild nature. Their physical activities have more to do with home repair and maintenance than camping safaris. They grow vegetables and flowers. For many artists, the lure was as much economic as it was scenic. These artists found themselves with growing families and a desire for what Cote called "non-defensive" living. Priced out of the Hamptons, unwilling to contend with the manicured Berkshires, they began filtering into the tired communities of the Hudson River Valley. Many teach at colleges in the region. Yet because they are artists and because they are responsive to light and setting, they make art out of their experiences in these places. By creating images prompted by the local environment, they have, without intending to, placed a new value on the ordinary landscape.

In the westward rolling days of the nineteenth century, artists were drawn to the epic and grandiose. The paintings of Albert Bierstadt, Frederic Church, and Worthington Whittredge, among many others, were reports about a land we did not know. We live in a less heroic age. Landscape painters of the Hudson River Valley are reporting now on a land we know but have not valued. How else to explain Marcia Clark's loving, lingering panorama of Poughkeepsie? Why would a painter who lives only half an hour from the Kaaterskill Clove choose to depict, instead, the view from her or his own backyard? Alexander Martin from New Paltz claims his work is "triggered off by the sky. The sky sets the whole mood." What difference does it make whether the sky is over Storm King Mountain or downtown Kingston?

Most of us do not live our lives at the edge of the Grand Canyon or in the deep hollows of Yosemite. We live in more ordinary settings, mixed environments, places which may, over time, reveal a different kind of beauty. Is it possible that artists whose values were shaped in urban environments are, when placed in rural settings, more tolerant of intrusive forms? Could it be that an artist from the city has learned to appreciate a different kind of nature, one that is less pristine, less wild, and more lived in?

What is emerging in the work of contemporary painters in the Hudson River Valley is a new definition of landscape beauty, one that requires a shift in our perceptions. What is beautiful in the landscape is what is healthy and sustainable. This ecological viewpoint encourages the appreciation of tidal wetlands, the preservation of architectural distinctiveness in small towns and the protection of modest-sized tributaries and streams. Mt. Marcy and the Tappan Zee are beautiful, of course, but so too are farm fields brought back into food production. Artists rarely see themselves as social activists, yet by their very choice of subject matter, they exert a formidable cultural force. By responding to the Hudson River Valley as it honestly is, by seeing life around them with clarity as well as love, the contemporary painters—the new natives—of the Hudson River Valley not only are enriching our aesthetic lives, but are also promoting the life-sustaining qualities of this unique region.

Catalogue of the Exhibition

Philip Allen

Known for his dramatically charged, mythic paintings, the artist not only reinvestigates the foundations of American Abstration, particularly the work of Pollock, de Kooning, and Gorky, but he has also found a way to synthesize their distinct approaches into an unmistakably personal mode. Images and paint coalesce. Restored to the act of painting after a long absence, imagination becomes, as it should be, a healing process. In a number of paintings done between 1980 and 1985, Allen transformed the grimness and isolation of urban life into a magical realm, where the sacred and profane are unified, and angels, tugboats, and fantastical creatures reside.

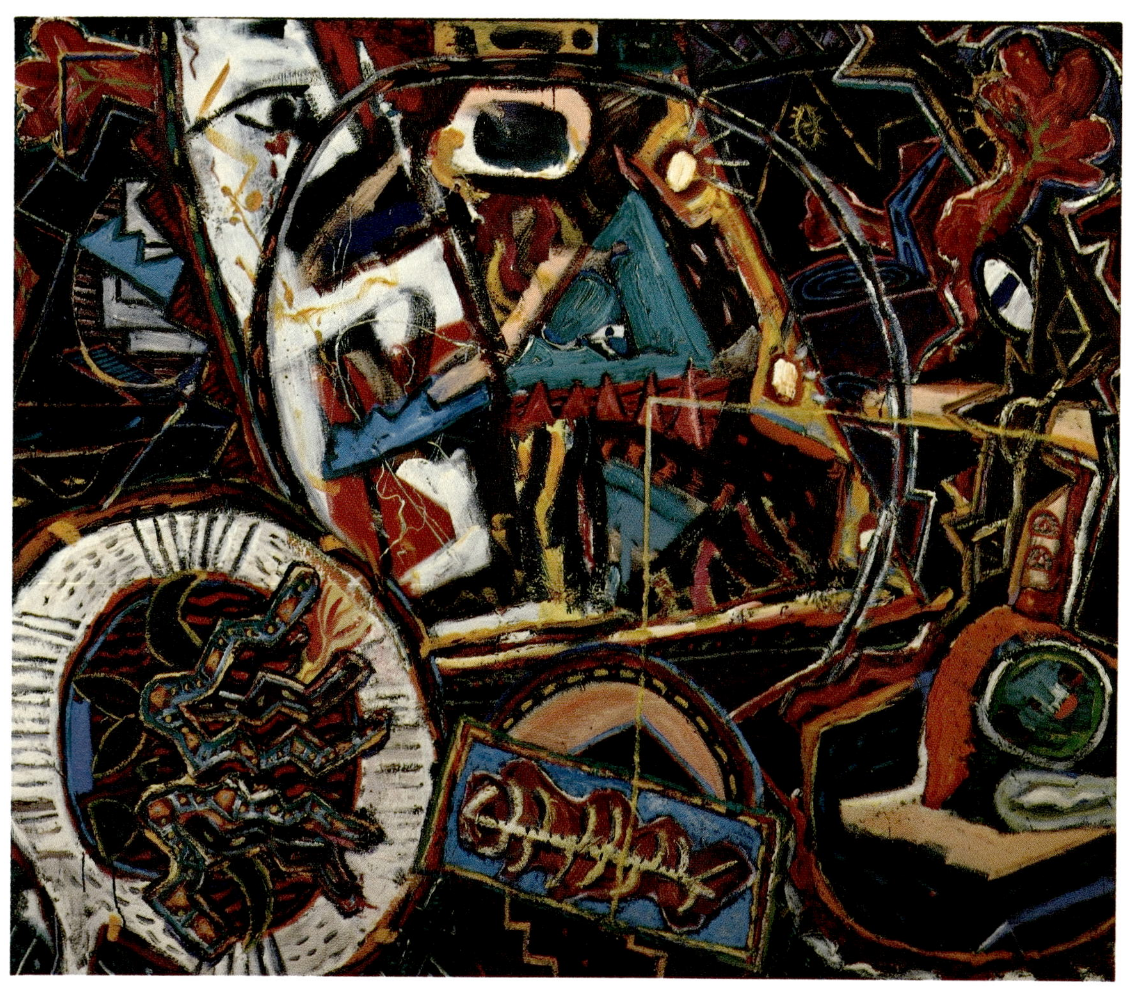

1

Night under the Bridge—East River
Oil on canvas, 1981
60 x 72 inches
Courtesy of the Equitable Life Assurance Society of the
United States

William Beckman

The artist is best known for his self-portraits and portraits. A narrative realist, he works at a slow and deliberate pace. On one level he is extremely committed to accurately transcribing a plenitude and range of visual information. On the other hand, his realism suggests a narrative possibility.

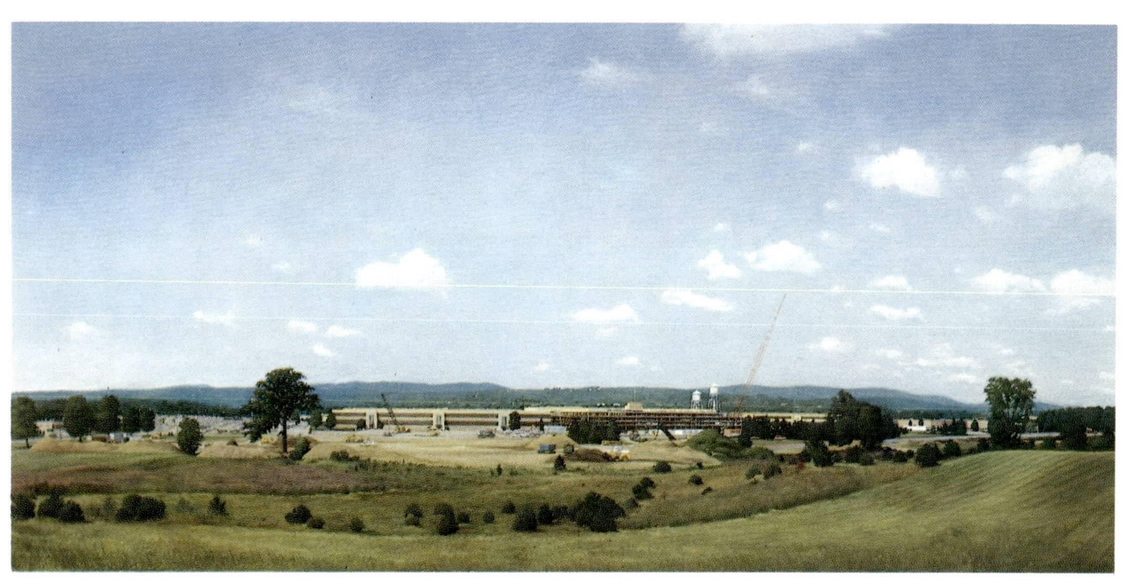

2

Construction on IBM Plant, Poughkeepsie
Pastel, 1983
40 x 82 inches
Courtesy Allan Frumkin Gallery

The artist first became known for his highly charged night scenes. Dark blues and inky blacks were used to form dense, impenetrable fields of color. Immersed in and contiguous with these dark, atmospheric grounds was a brightly lit house at the edge of a forest, a country road winding through the mountains, or a deserted office building towering above an empty street. Berlind's continuing preoccupation with the possibilities of juxtaposition has recently led him to depict an eerily lit dock on a lake at night, and romantic, purple clouds scudding across a pink, backlit sky above a section of industrial blight along the Hudson River. Rather than attempting to force a connection among the disparate elements, Berlind employs a unified painterly approach to explore the subtle differences. Color, tone, light, shape, perspective, and brushstroke are all made to contribute to the overall composition.

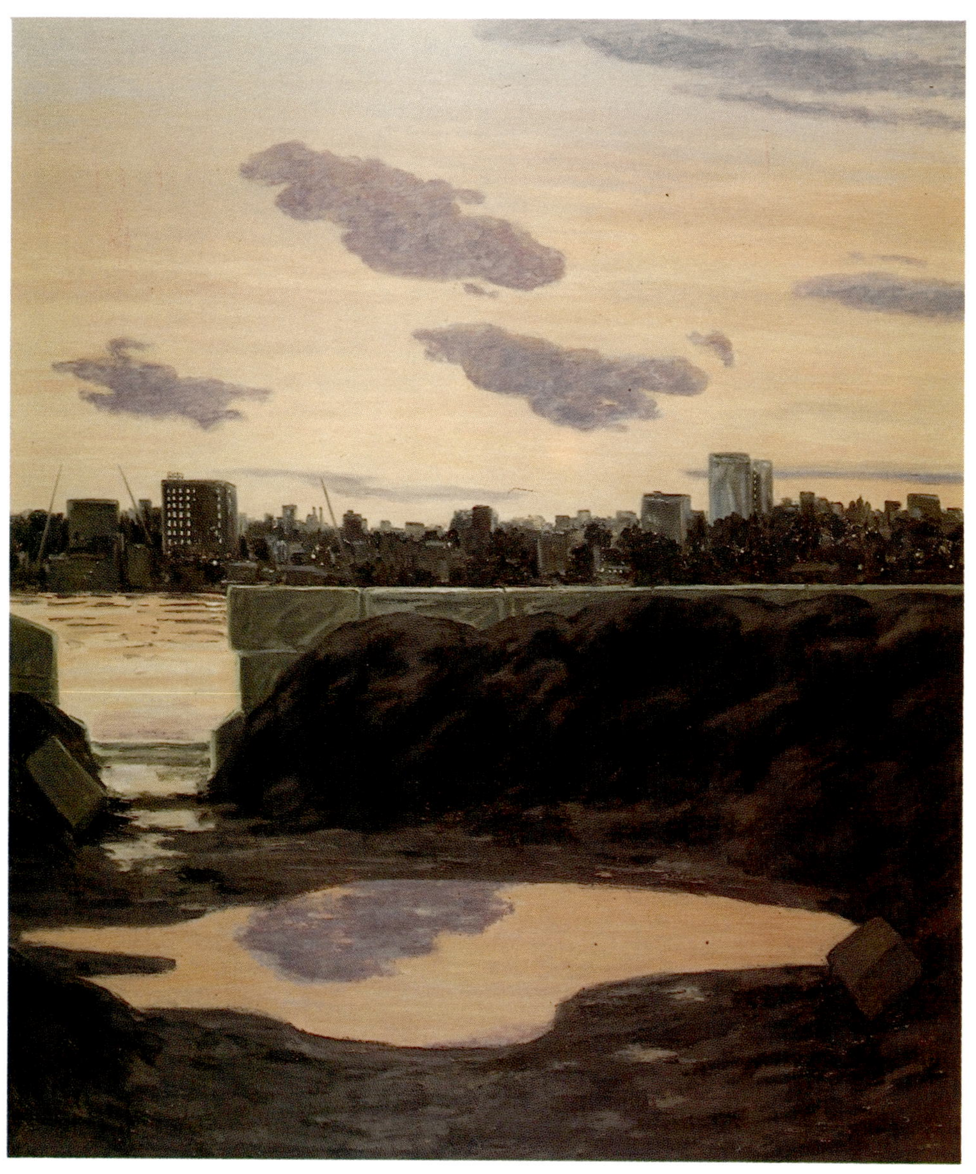

3

Sudden Slowness
Oil on canvas, 1984
84 x 72 inches
Couresy of Ruth Siegel Ltd.

Robert Birmelin

The artist's moody cityscapes and confrontational views of crowded urban streets evolve out of direct observation filtered through memory and imagination. The cityscapes are, for example, fluent composites of places Birmelin sees while driving into Manhattan from New Jersey, where he and his family live. Whether it is a hot summer sky permeated by a scarlet sunset and smoke billowing from a blazing building, or a long view of office buildings, warehouses, tenements, and a traffic-filled highway along the Hudson River at dusk, the paintings are imbued with the emotional tenor of urban life. Light and atmosphere are depicted as both events and traces of our interior life.

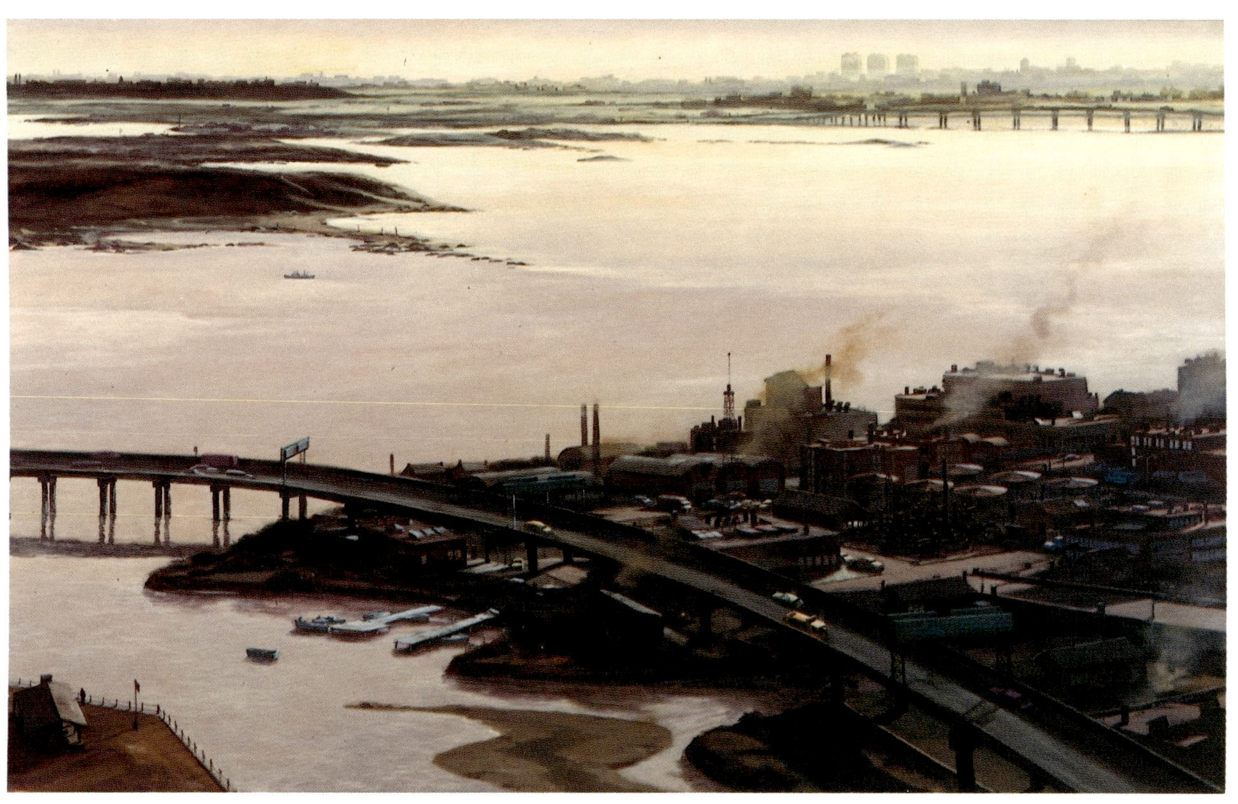

4

Cityscape, River with Industry
Acrylic on canvas, 1984
48 x 78 inches
Sherry French Gallery

Marcia Clark

In a statement made in May 1983, the artist wrote: "It was the 19th century painter Thomas Cole and other 19th century artists with their close observations that set me on my present course. I was already painting landscape, but looking at Cole landscapes in particular, the paintings were saying, 'Are you looking? Well look deeper. Are you recording what you see? Well clarify that focus. There's more and it's possible to make it manifest!' The drawings amplified on this and the writings were equally eloquent, appealing both to the vision and the imagination."

Around the time this statement was made, Clark began working in far larger formats, while maintaining her keen interest in panoramic views and peripheral vision. In having the views spill beyond the composition's borders, the artist confronts the viewer with a world that is physical as well as visual. The scene stretches, curves, or drops away, reminding the viewer that the world is as much an act of seeing and feeling as it is an aggregate of objects in space.

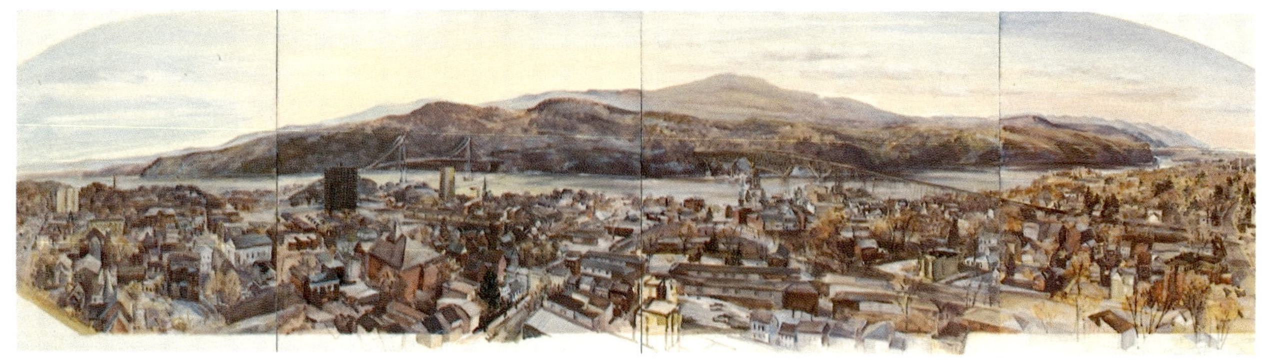

5

Quartet
Oil on birch panel, 1985
25 x 84 inches
Courtesy of the Artist

Arthur Cohen

The intimate paintings of Arthur Cohen, a painterly realist
who has been carefully and quietly honing his craft for
more than 25 years, can be scrupulously delicate, convincingly naturalistic, or broadly gestural. This deceptive
lack of style should suggest the artist's relentless desire to
get at his subject matter from every conceivable angle. In
his paintings of Provincetown and the Brooklyn Bridge —
his two favorite subjects — he uses color and brushwork
to evoke the time of day and weather, set a mood, or place
in perfect counterpoint the tiny and the expansive, the
heroic and humble.

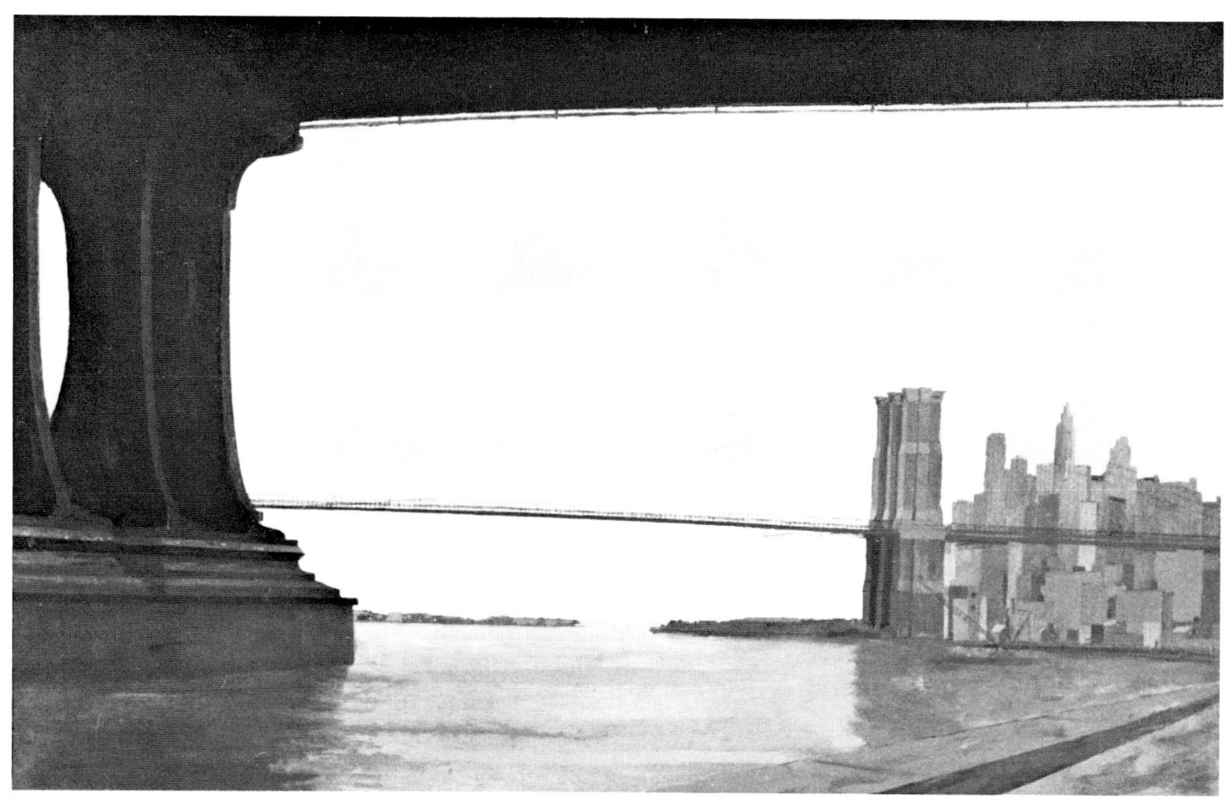

6

Brooklyn Bridge Sunset
Acrylic on canvas, 1984
30 x 48 inches
David Findlay, Jr., Inc.

Alan Cote

The artist lives and works in a converted factory building overlooking the Rondout in Kingston. Rather than being derived from direct observation, Cote's highly mediated, allusive abstractions can be said to evolve out of his deeply personal absorption of the surrounding landscape. In command of a large, supple vocabulary of shapes, line, and color, he is capable of evoking the Hudson River's moonlit surface in as simple and dramatic a form as a lone bird juxtaposed against a sooty pink sky. Committed to extending the principles of High Modernism, the artist has found a way to transform the presence of nature into the realm of paint. The viewer is confronted by a vision that is expansive and intimate, revelatory and introspective.

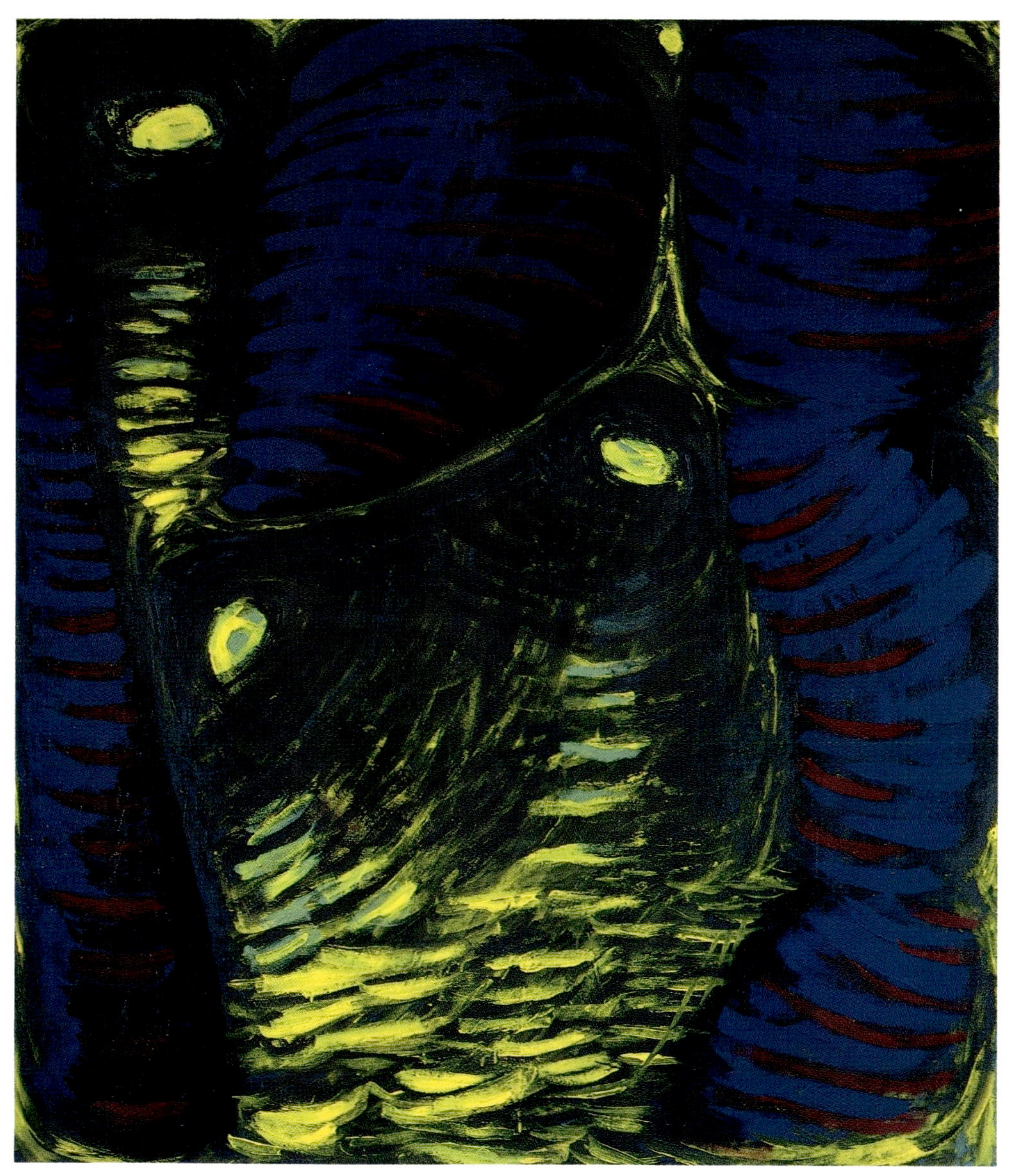

7a

Lights on the Water at Night
Acrylic on canvas, 1982
72 x 64 inches
Courtesy of Washburn Gallery

b

Anticipation of the Waterfall (Not illustrated)
Acrylic on canvas, 1982
72 x 108 inches
Courtesy of Washburn Gallery

David Coughtry

Scrupulous to the point of calling to mind Ansel Adams'
photographs, Coughtry's paintings are naturalistic, obses-
sive, and precise. Delicate brushwork and subtle tonal
gradations are carefully manipulated tools of description.
Specificity is the key. Paint is a way to transform the visible
world into a meticulous surface of contemplation and
wonder.

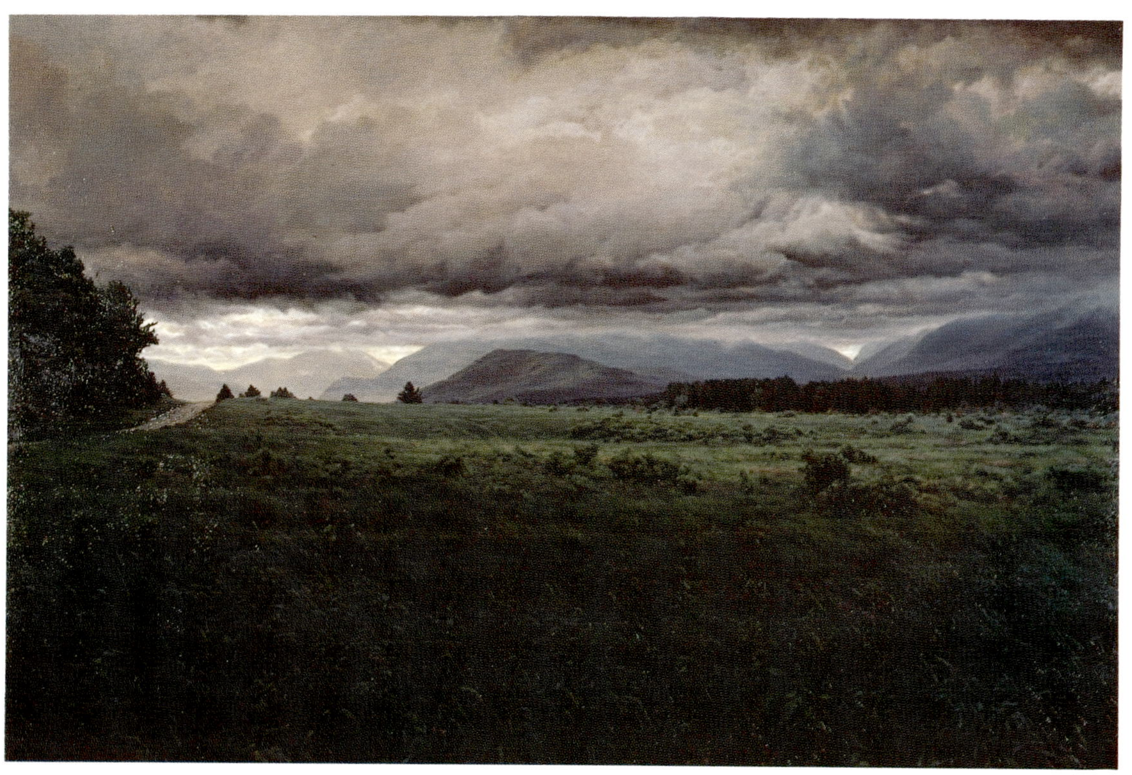

8

North Elba
Oil on canvas, 1984
46 x 70 inches
Collection Albany Institute of History and Art

Jagged edges, rounded shapes, and linear elements form the basis of the artist's abstract vocabulary. The impulse behind the paintings is to evoke a mythic view of the landscape. By transforming the visible world with its plenitude of details into simple yet specific shapes and flat areas of color, Creighton is able to depict the rhythmic relationship between hills and clouds or the stark outline of a branch against an expansive sky. The compositions are comprised of carefully orchestrated counterpoints between vertical and horizontal, line and shape, dark and light.

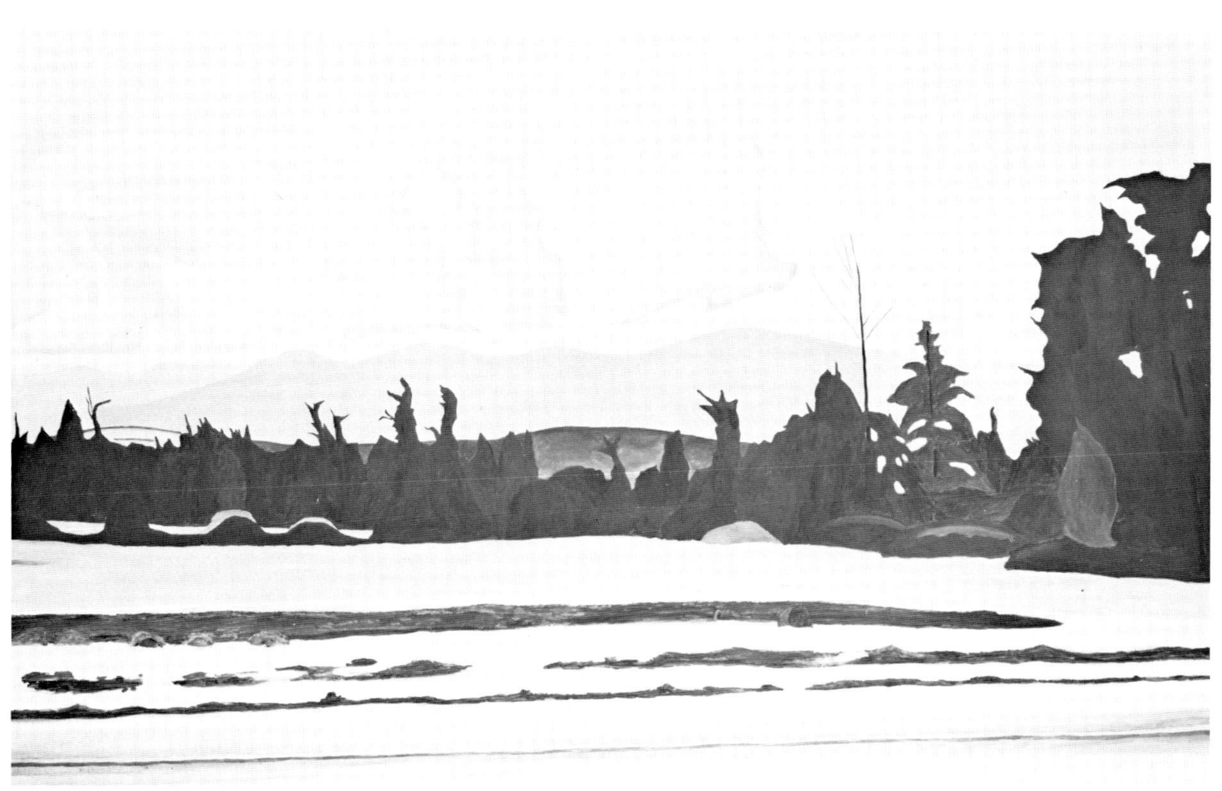

9

Catskill Petit Four
Oil on canvas, 1984
36 x 56 inches
Lent by the Artist

Joseph DiGiorgio

The artist is intensely preoccupied with the way light and atmosphere permeate as well as define a landscape. Highly sensitive to the nuances of light and effects of shadow, he can go from registering the subtlest tonal shifts to laying down a shimmering optical field in the same painting. Derived from both Pointillism and recent abstraction, DiGiorgio's lozenge-shaped abstract mark can function as a solid shape, atmospheric accent, and condition of light simultaneously. Seen as reflection, solid body, rippling surface, and dispersal of bits of color, the river's surface is transformed into an awe-filled realm of seeing and feeling.

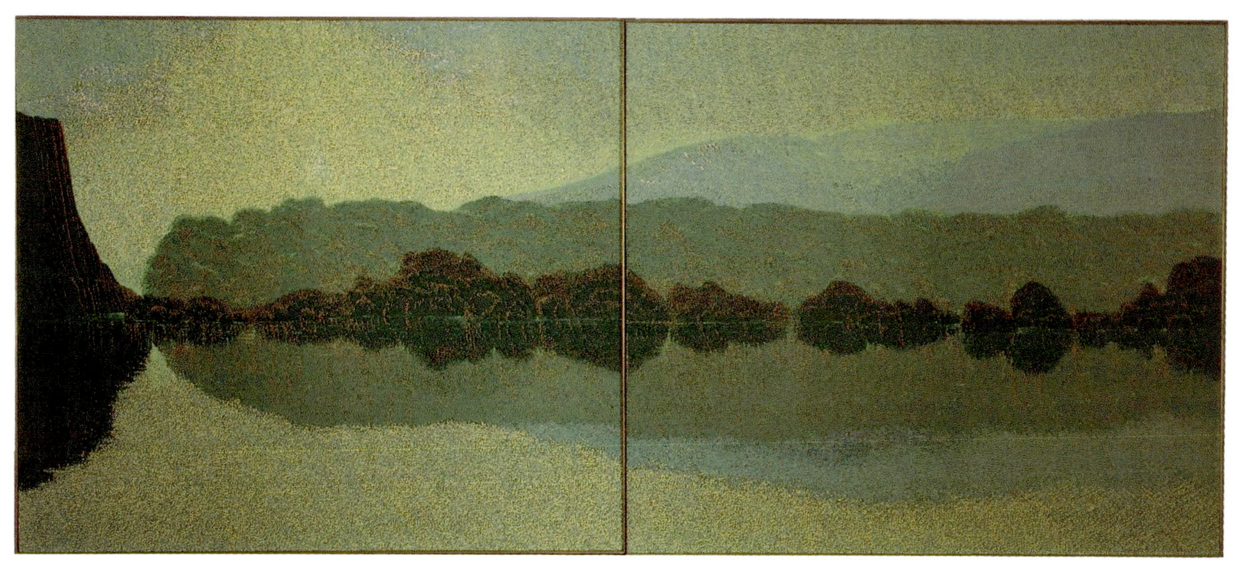

10

Hudson River, Number 6
Oil on canvas, 1982
72 x 168 inches
Courtesy of Ruth Siegel Ltd.

Rackstraw Downes

Since the late 1960s, this English-born artist has been committed to depicting panoramic views within narrow, horizontal formats. His tightly controlled compositions are notable for their range of details, attention to light, plainness of subject matter, and sweeping views. Underscoring all of this is Downes' highly evolved theory of optics: the scenes seem to bend around the viewer, while, at the same time, following and even emphasizing the curve of the horizon. Focusing on what is in front of him as well as at the edges of his peripheral vision, Downes' compositions will drop away suddenly at the edges of the painting. The act of seeing becomes a physical probing of the world, rather than a passive receiving of stimuli.

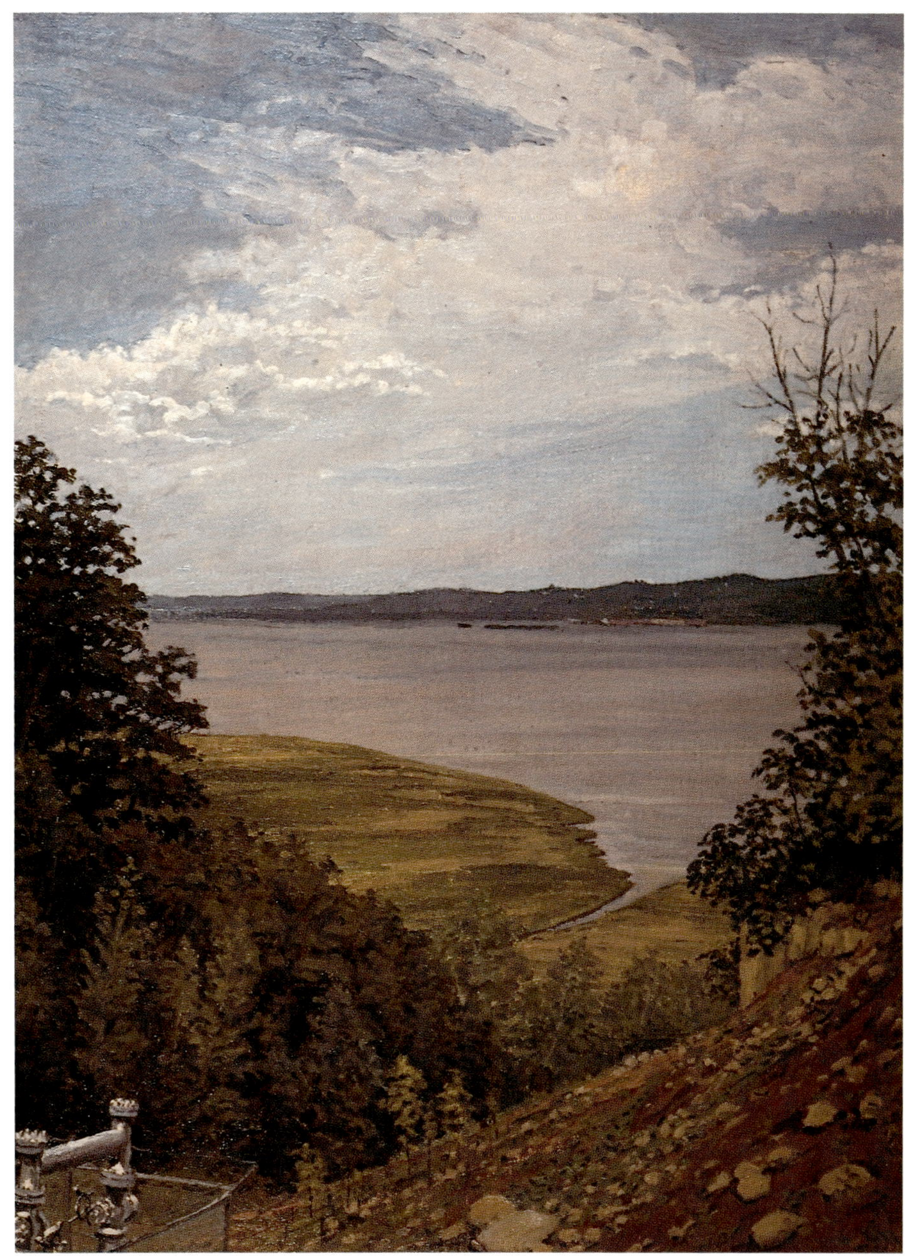

11

Nyack
Oil on canvas, 1973
29 7/16 x 22 inches
Courtesy of Claude Bernard Gallery Ltd.

Katherine Doyle

The artist was born in San Francisco, studied art, art history, and literature in Europe, and finally settled in Florence. She travels often to the United States for her subjects, many of which she finds in the Hudson River Valley. Her work is preoccupied with a detailed examination of the effects of weather and light on water and vegetation. Her strong background in Academic methods of painting can be clearly seen in the painstakingly precise style she has evolved.

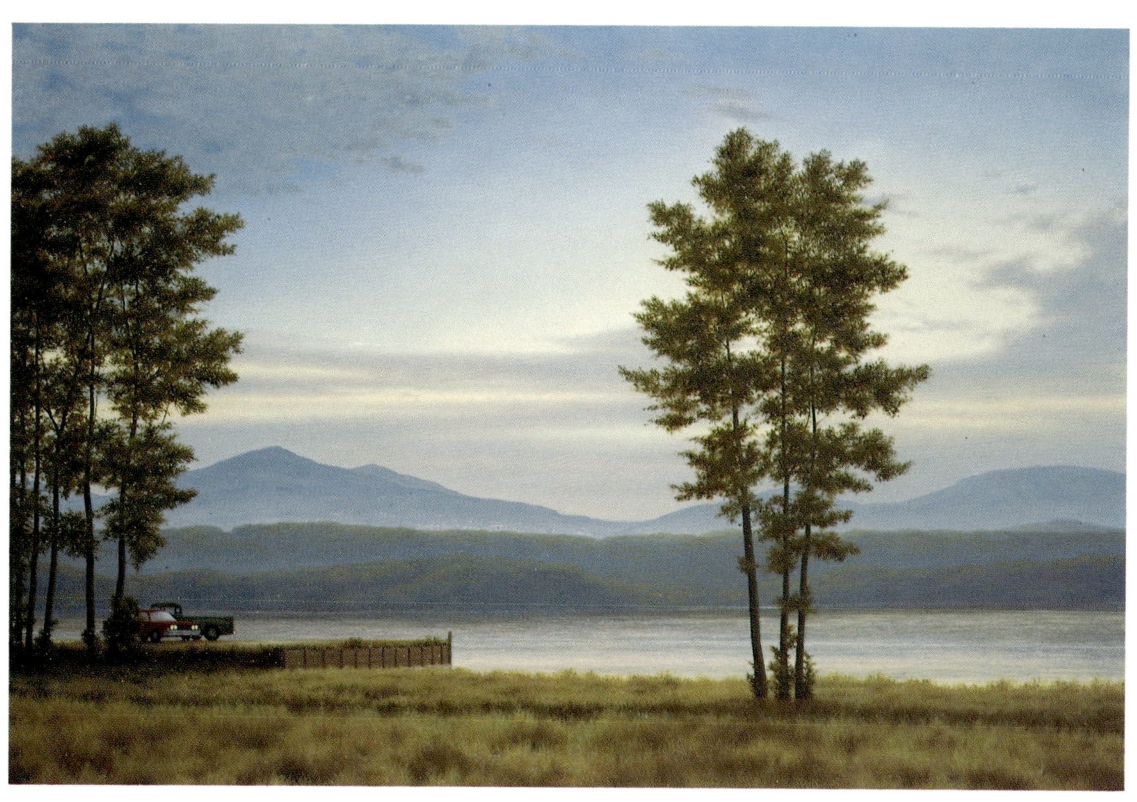

12

Landing Stage Near Stuyvesant, N.Y.
Oil on canvas, 1985
24 x 36 inches
Courtesy David Findlay Jr., Inc.

Alan Gussow

Statement made by him on August 31, 1985

For many years I was a landscape painter. My paintings were characterized by active brushwork (a holdover from my days as a student during the height of abstract expressionism) and by a feeling for local color. These pictures emphasized the texture of a place rather than realistic appearances. In the nineteen seventies the paintings found inspiration in what I was doing rather than what I was seeing. What I did then was garden—plant, dig, taste, harvest and listen to birds and insects. These works were more abstract than the landscape paintings, though I believed they gained a greater reality by giving visible form to a full range of sense experiences—what I was hearing, smelling, tasting and touching, as well as what I was seeing.

In the nineteen eighties, prompted by a trip to Australia and my first contact with aboriginal art, I began to carve, cut and sew pieces—all in an effort to invoke both a greater physical presence and to suggest ritual possibilities. I also began a series of site-specific ceremonial offerings in Texas, California, Oregon, Colorado, Maine and on Long Island. During this period, I also initiated my art and anti-nuclear actions, culminating in the International Shadow Project. I am now designing sets and lighting for a dance company and am working as a design consultant on a Peace Park installation planned for a National Park Service site on the west coast.

My more private art continues, however. The piece in this exhibition, **Welcome to the Kaaterskill Falls**, is characteristic of my work since 1981, with one difference; this is the first time I have used chalk on such a large scale. What I am attempting to do in my work now is to locate a reality which animates tribal art and to find an appropriate formal language which will enable my work to function in this society with the same sense of ritual, ceremony and meaning that it continues to do among so-called primitive (primal) peoples. My return to the Kaaterskill Clove was prompted by a desire to re-establish a connection with both the place itself and with Thomas Cole, whose response to this location served to mark the beginning of the Hudson River School of painting. It was important to me to make the first cuts in the fabric on location, to work directly from the site; it was equally necessary that I hang the work there so that the air and wetness surrounding the falls could blow through my piece. Working with chalk in my studio allowed me to sustain a tactile connection with the place. I think of this piece as a banner for the Clove, an analog to the kind of banners small towns hang across their main street announcing a fireman's fair. This piece might have been prepared by native American Indians as a sign of welcome to Cole, Durand and the rest, or at least so I imagine. In that sense, I position myself in a cross-cultural context, clearly not an Indian and equally, not a member of a nineteenth century brotherhood, but rather somewhere in between, introducing one group to the other.

Congers, New York

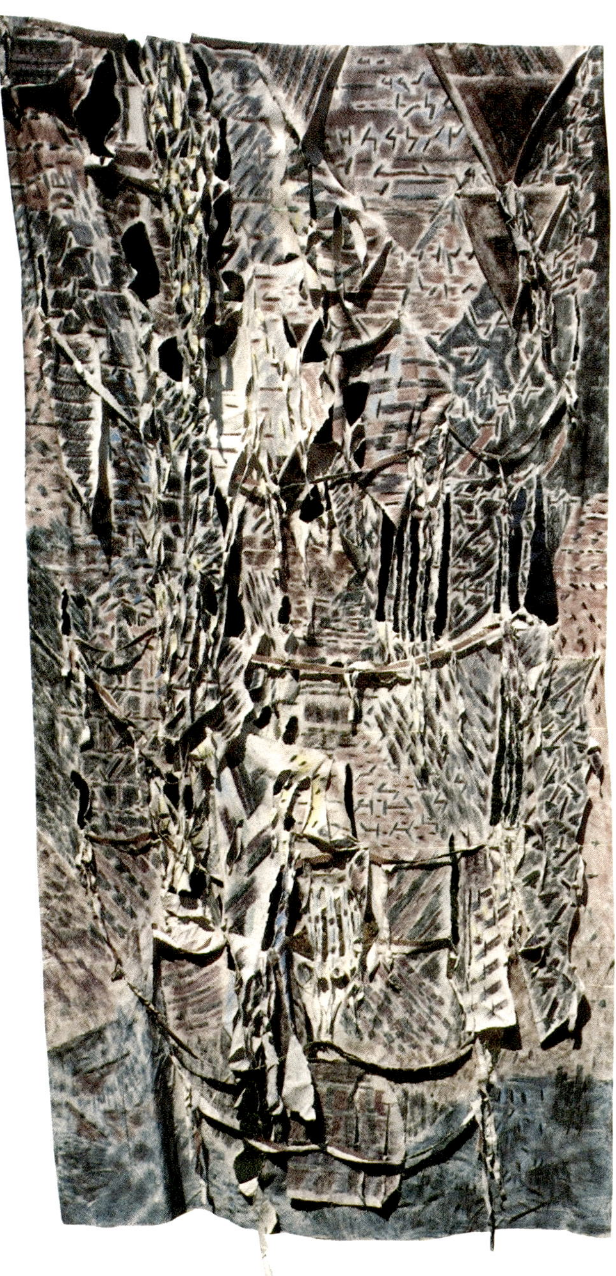

13

Welcome to Kaaterskill Falls
Cotton duck, cut and sewn, with chalk and acrylic
1985
12 x 6 ft.
Lent by the Artist

Yvonne Jacquette

In order to depict expansive aerial views of the city at night, Jacquette circles above such places as San Francisco, Manhattan, and Tokyo in a plane or helicopter. The busyness below is transformed into a stately vision of order and gracefulness. Viewers are apt to feel as if they are suspended above a bridge, office buildings, noisy streets, nuclear plants, or entwined necklaces of headlights snaking their way past the city limits. Night is seen as a sensual, black field in which constellations of jewel-like lights have been placed. A brightly lit bridge can loop across a glistening river, while rows of high-rises form geometric patterns of light. The artist chooses her angles of vision with a quietly dramatic flair. The paintings are as mysterious, romantic, and alluring as night itself.

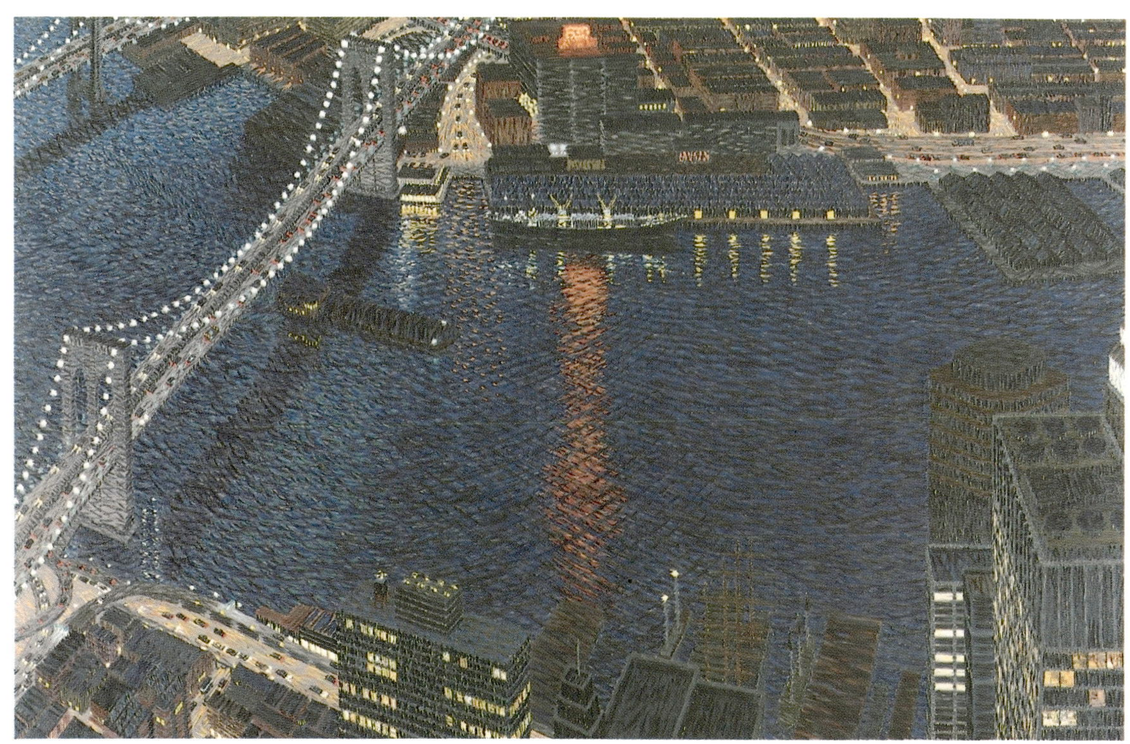

14a

**East River View with Brooklyn Bridge
(Not included in Exhibition)**
Oil on Canvas, 1983
96 x 128 inches
Courtesy of the Brooklyn Museum

b

**East River Night (with Brooklyn Bridge) III
(Not illustrated)**
Pastel on paper, 1982
27 x 32 inches
Courtesy of Mr. Morton Landowne

Among the widely different series of paintings Jones has completed in the last few years is a group depicting the Hudson River and Lower Manhattan at sunset. The views are angled down from an elevated section of the West Side Highway. Cars, buses, and trucks are parked along the water's edge. The factory buildings and warehouses on the other side take on a portentous air. Color is garish and expressive. The light reflected off the river is alluring yet demonic. The viewer is confronted by a dark vision of urban isolation and despair.

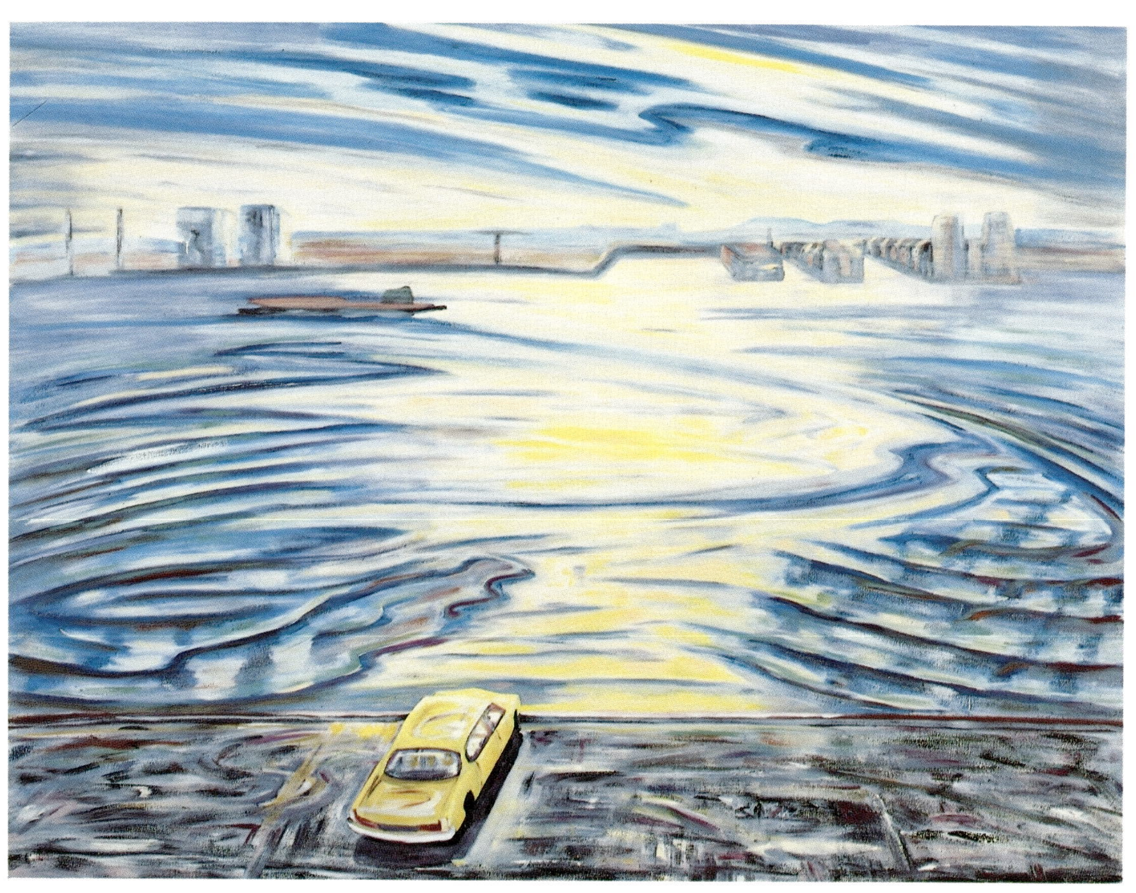

15

Good Government
Oil on canvas, 1980
54 x 72 inches
Lent by the Artist

Arnold Levine

In a letter to one of the curators of this exhibition, the artist stated: "The painting *Poughkeepsie From The West Bank Of The Hudson* was painted on a clear still day. I tried to do a straightforward painting just as I viewed it. It was finished in just a couple of sittings." Nervous, fragile strokes crystallize the scene. Although the artist is concerned with a literal transcription of the observed scene, he is also interested in the possibilities of a painterly approach.

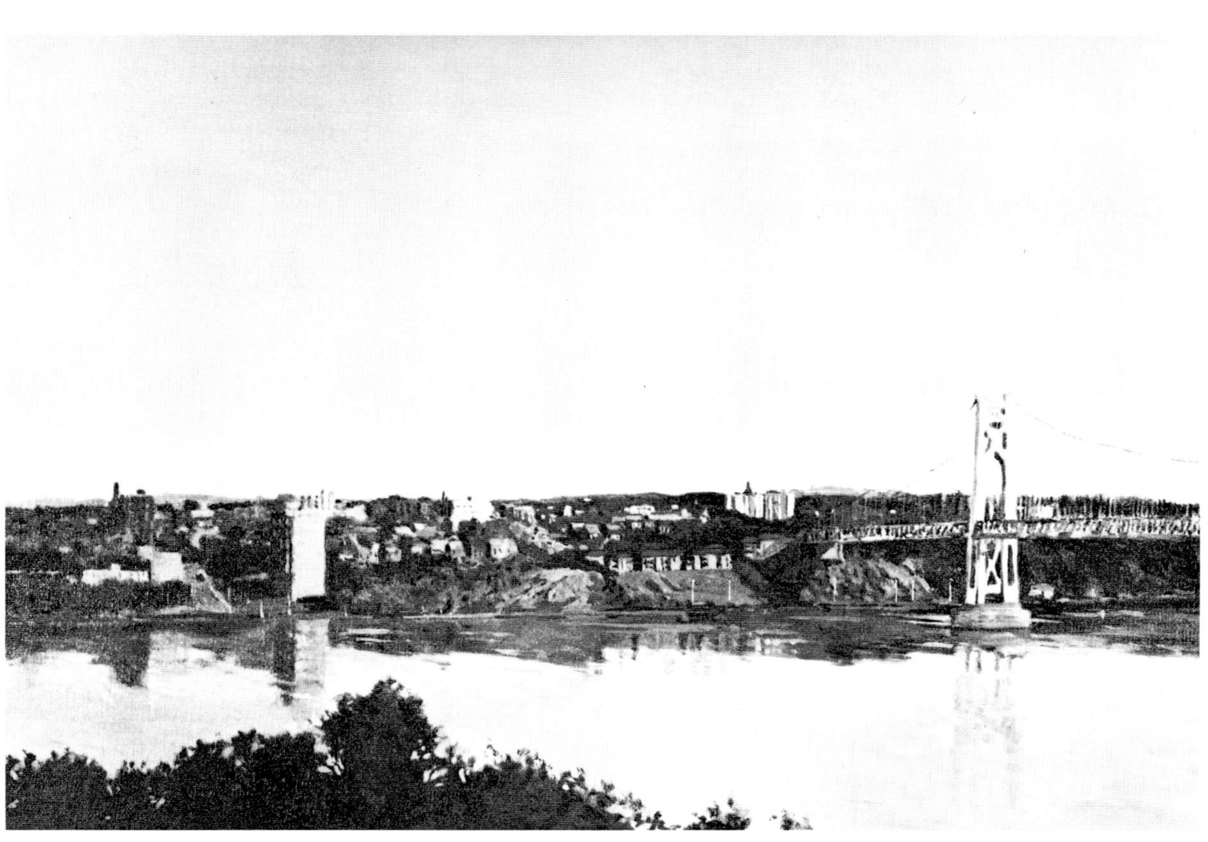

16

Poughkeepsie from the West Bank of the Hudson
Oil on canvas, 1981
16 x 24 inches
Private collection

Alex Martin

The dominant feature of Alex Martin's paintings is a cloud-filled sky. Color, shape, transparent layers, active brush-work, and a sense of relentless movement are used to convey the impact of a moment, rather than a place. Columns of clouds twist, disperse, scurry, rush, gather, or quietly preside over the landscape. Aspects of representation and abstraction have been synthesized in an emotionally convincing manner.

Born on a dairy farm outside Kinderhook, Martin returned to the Hudson River Valley during the middle 1960s, and has lived there ever since. The move played a significant role in the artist's thinking. "I felt strong connections of moving back to where I was born. All my childhood images came back. I remembered the patterns of light in the woods, the dry grass, the big farm spaces. I remember going down the river on milk runs with my father to meet the *20th Century Limited* in Albany, and the dark, dramatic clouds over the Catskills. These early associations were magical—full of mystery and excitement for me."

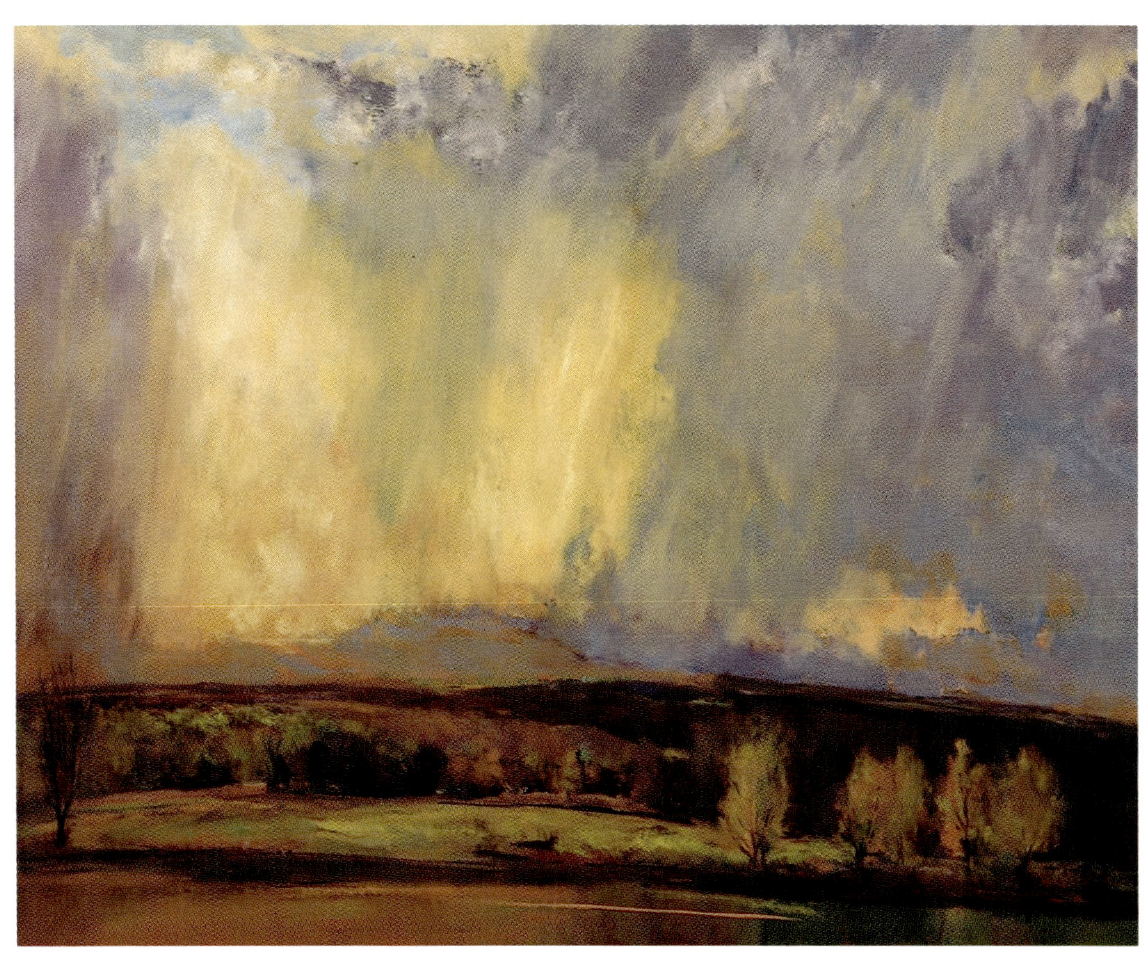

17

Toward Mohonk, Early Spring
Oil on canvas, 1985
48 x 60 inches
Lent by the artist

Nancy Mitchnick

The artist's paintings radiate with an emotional and physical directness. Their heavily impastoed surfaces shimmer with voluptuous color and juicy light. Although Mitchnick is neither methodical in her juxtapositions of color nor mystical in her attitudes toward nature, her work seems to pick up where Fauvism and German Expressionism left off. The stinging lushness results from her staccato brushstrokes of hot color and thick paint. Like a jazz drummer, the artist jabs, hammers, squeezes, scrapes, layers, and caresses her subject matter, until it is transformed into an ode to the pleasures of both seeing and painting.

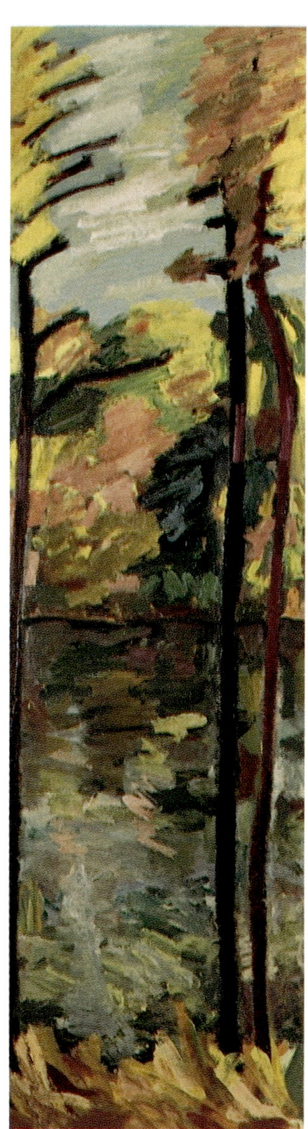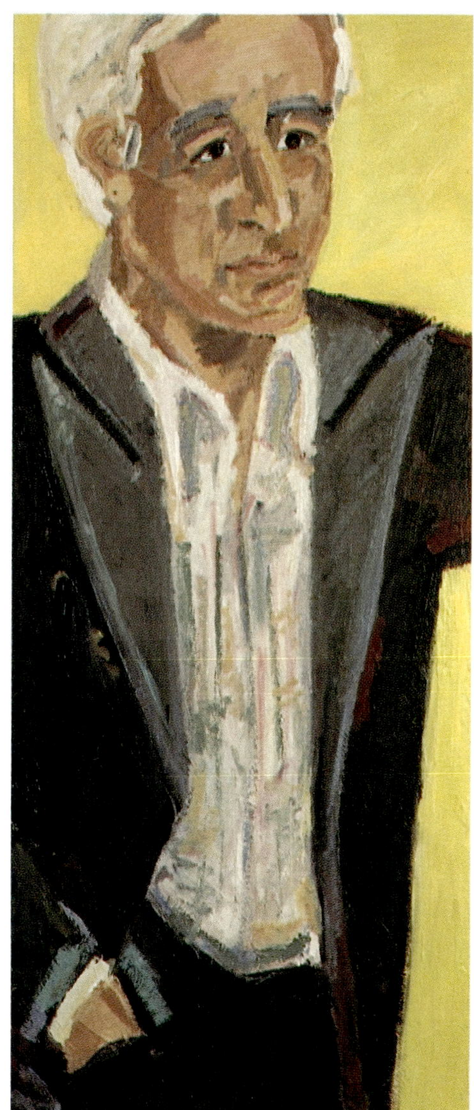

18

Dr. Wolff/Loon Lake
Oil on canvas, 1985
84 x 60 inches
Courtesy of Hirschl & Adler Modern

Catherine Murphy

The artist possesses the rare strength to gaze unflinchingly at the world around her. The paintings are celebrated for their scrupulous attention to the subtlest shift in light and tone, as well as their confrontation with the harsh presence of the city she lives in—its factories, rundown buildings, dramatic contrasts between parks and office buildings, interior and exterior views. Murphy's realist vision exists somewhere between a compulsive need to be factual and disquieting hallucination. The paintings examine the world, rather than observe it. It's as if everything is seen for the first time, in all its wonder and grimness. The ordinary reaches a weird, extraordinary pitch.

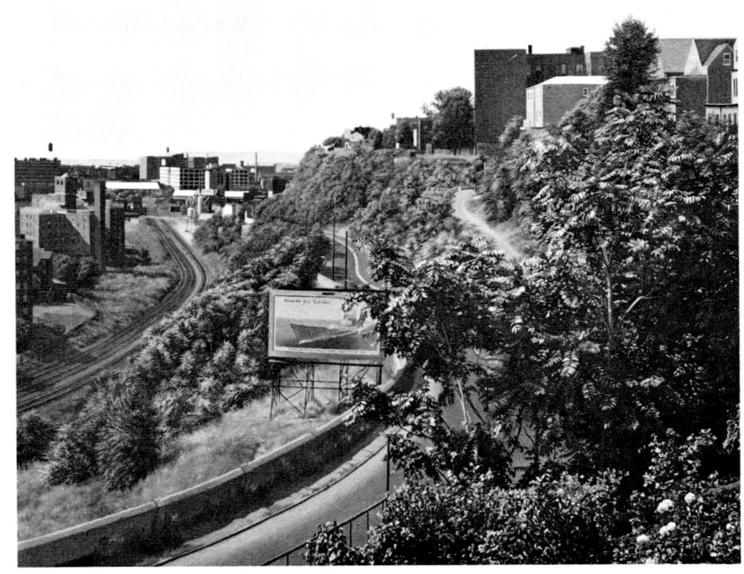

Ailanthus Trees (Not in exhibition)
Oil on canvas, 1975
26⅞ x 35 inches
Collection of Mr. and Mrs. Herbert Landau

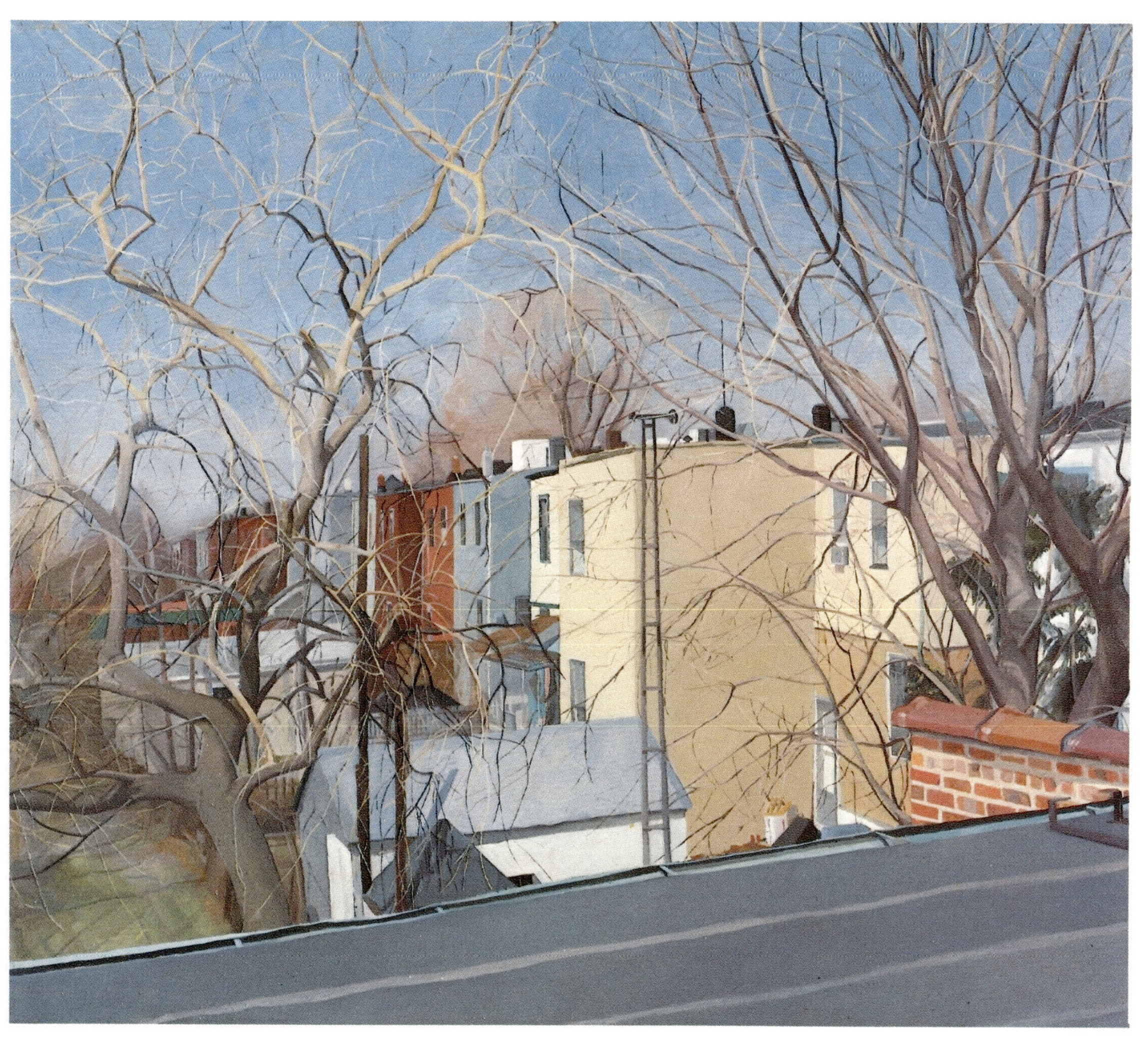

19

Backyards, Jamaica, New York
Oil on canvas, 1970
39 x 45 inches
Courtesy New Jersey State Museum

Andrew Needle

The artist's work derives its charm from its choice of homely scenes. The locale is never too specific, allowing the viewers to feel they might have experienced the scenes themselves. One of Needle's most interesting compositional devices is his use of sharp, bare tree branches to organize the rectangle of the painting's format. The branches hold the picture's surface taut, while the loose, gestural background becomes an invitation for the viewer to look past and through these obstructions. The theme of obstruction is pushed even further by the outcropping of rocks in the foreground. Consequently, we feel that we are both in the painting and looking at it from the outside.

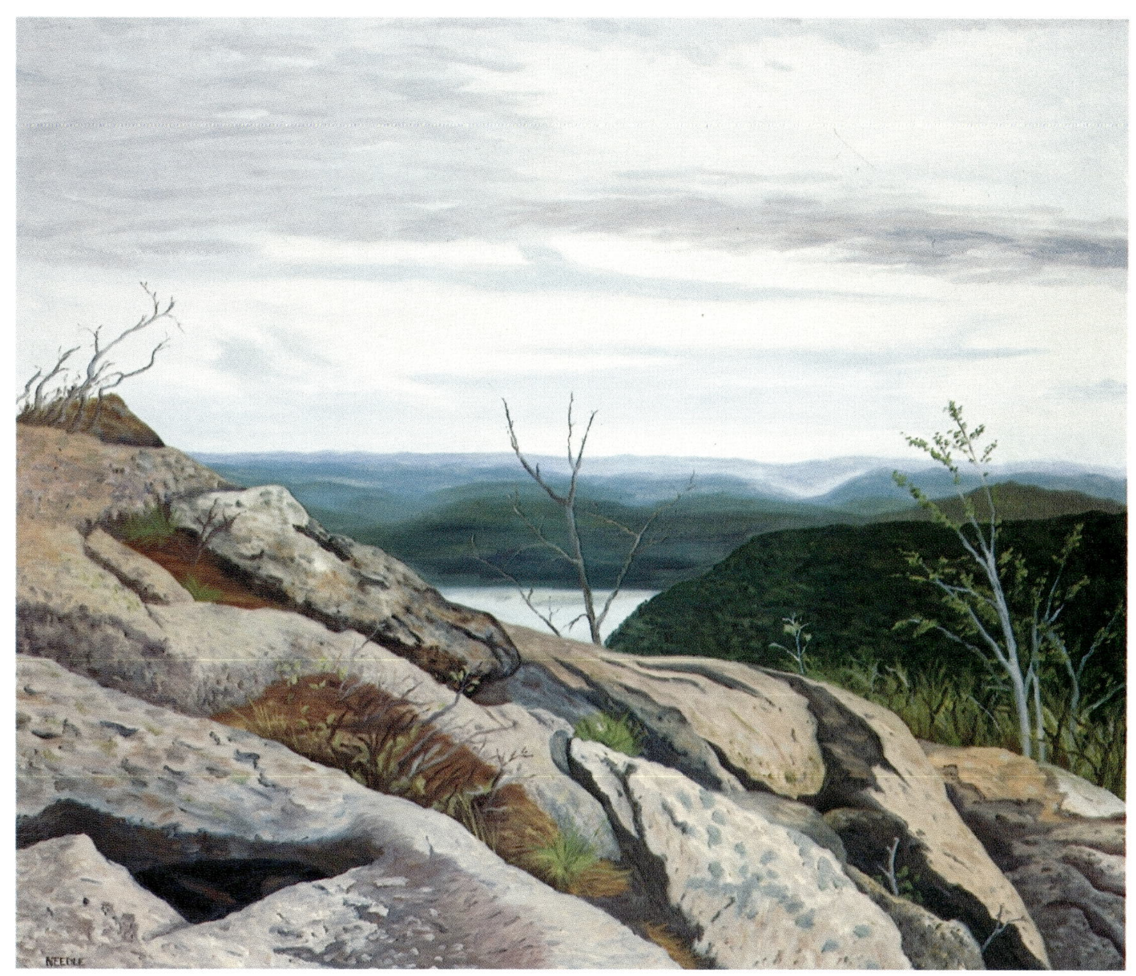

20

Bear Mountain Lookout
Oil on canvas, 1985
40 x 48 inches
Lent by the Artist

Ross Neher

Ross Neher displayed a remarkable artistic talent while growing up in West Camp (Ulster County) and was encouraged to study with various artists who lived in nearby Woodstock. The paintings and watercolors he did as a young boy convey a mature understanding of the formal aspects of composition. An early love for the surrounding landscape—he could see the Catskill Mountains from his parents' home—and an admiration for the Hudson River School continue to play a significant role in the work of this abstract artist.

Although his shapes, colors, and tonal shifts allude to the landscape of his childhood, the paintings must be seen as highly mediated, contemplative abstractions. The light emanating from the depths of their smooth, buttery surfaces is metaphysical rather than descriptive. Evolving out of the Visionary tradition of 19th century American landscape painting, Neher has developed a deeply personal vocabulary within the formal limits of Modernist abstraction. An intense, interior life is made visible.

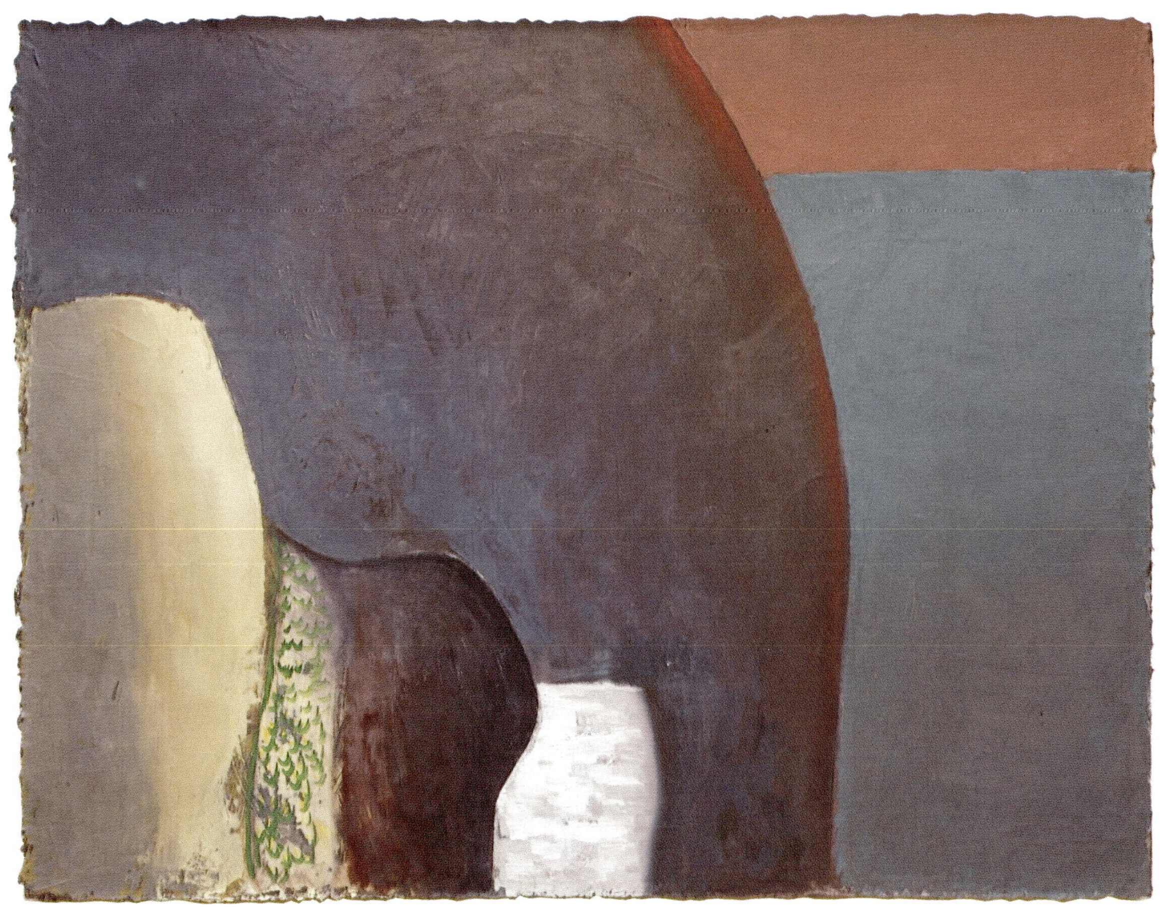

21a   b

West Camp
Oil on linen, 1985
36 x 48 inches
Lent by the Artist

The Watch (Not shown)
Oil on linen, 1985
36 x 48 inches
Lent by the Artist

Don Nice

About his ongoing project, *Hudson River Series*, the artist has said: "The Hudson River Works all have that stereotype vista look that has become in itself an American icon, a postcard emotion that is very familiar." This approach is "in direct contrast to the Hudson River School, in which each new painting brought to the world a vision of a paradise lost and a new extension of the sublime."

The paintings are usually landscape vistas which incorporate individual depictions of objects along the work's base. While the placement of the images can be seen as a modern use of the Renaissance *predella,* the narrative current implied by the choice of the objects is both contemporary and understated. A flashlight, sneaker, crumpled coke can, popcorn bag, and sunglasses imply the tourist's accessories and refuse. A squirrel, blue jay, and bear, on the other hand, allude to the area's wildlife. Found in and around the landscape that is the central focus of the painting, the groups of objects, animals, fruits, and vegetables form separate commentaries on man's relationship to his surroundings.

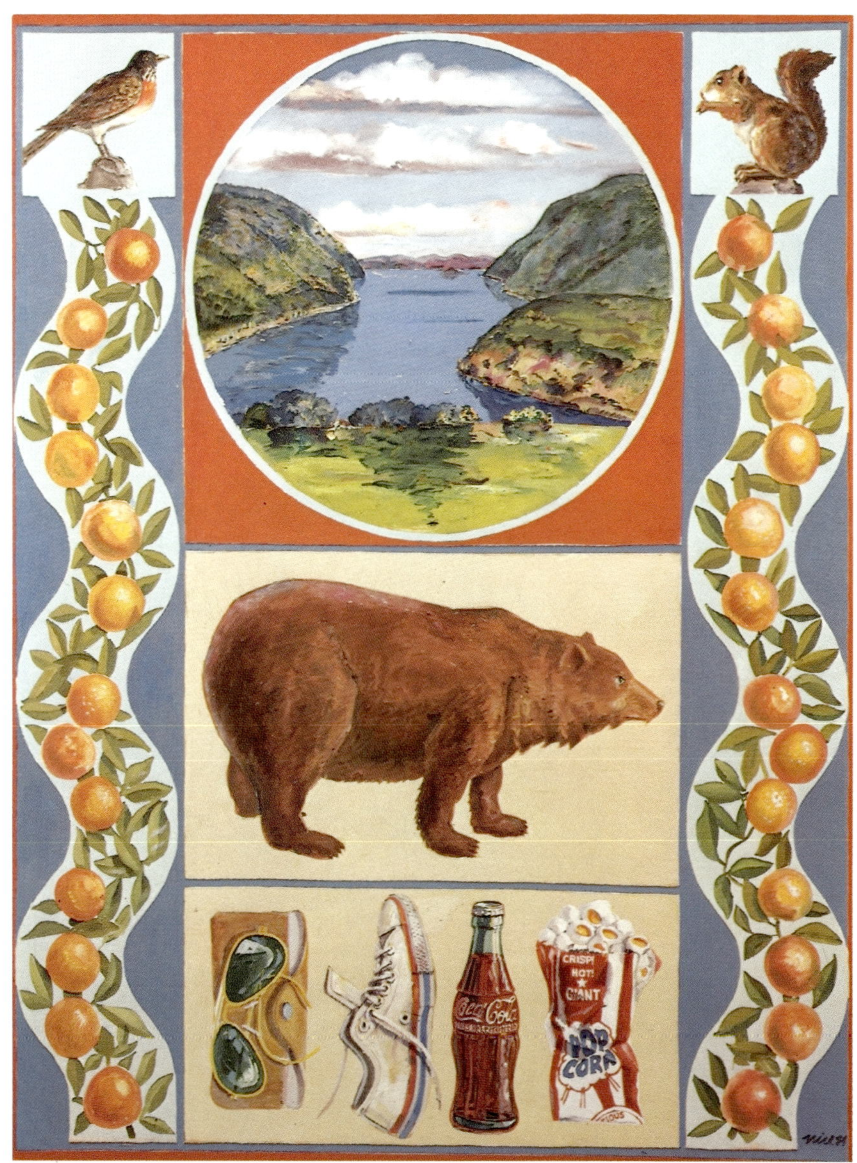

22

Bear Totem
Oil on canvas, 1984
75¼ x 57 inches
Courtesy of Nancy Hoffman Gallery

Henry Orlyk

As a child growing up in Cohoes, the artist became sensitive to all the different kinds of upstate winters. A tonalist,
he keeps his palette restrained and colors muted. The
subtle interplay of horizontal and vertical brushstrokes
weaves the painting together. Silence in all its forms is
made visible.

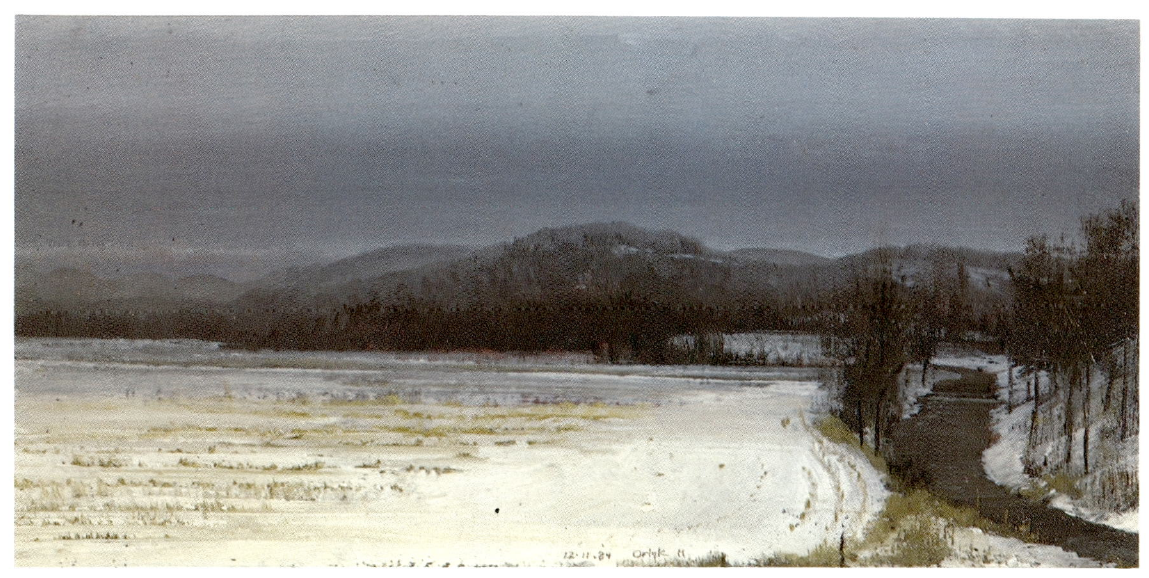

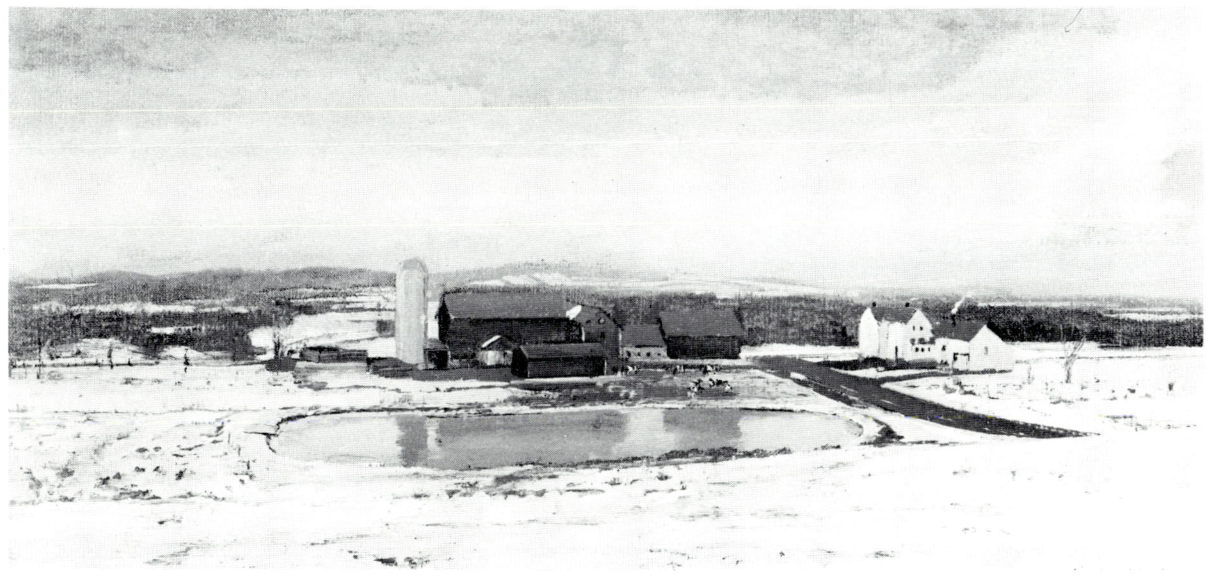

23a   **b**

Edge of a Cornfield   **Frozen Pond, Rice Farm**
Oil on canvas, 1984   Oil on canvas, 1985
10 x 21 inches   10 x 22½ inches
Private collection   Private collection

Richard Pitts

The artist employs a painterly approach to revitalize a familiar image of 19th century American landscape painting. At the same time, he manages to avoid making either an ironic pastiche or a nostalgic icon. Quietness suffuses throughout, and an intense longing for a calmer world is convincingly conveyed.

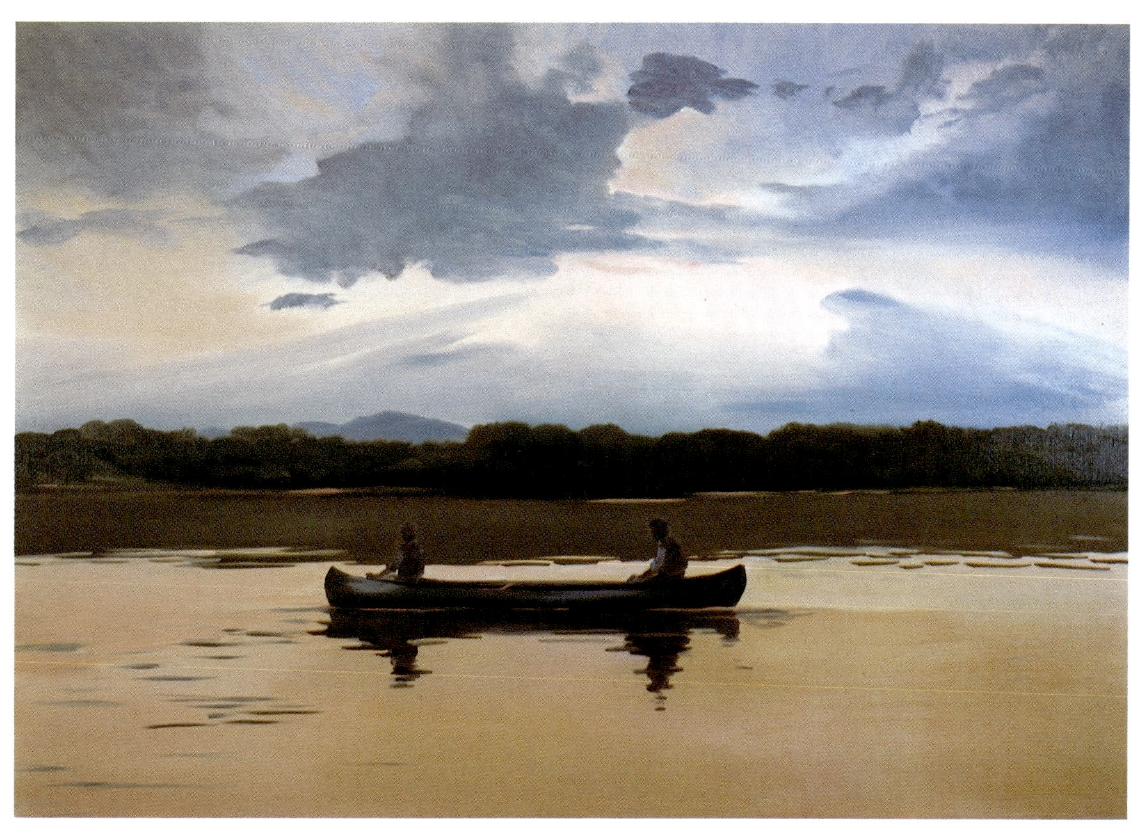

24

Hudson River
Oil on canvas, 1985
50 x 72 inches
Lent by the Artist

Anne Poor

The artist has lived most of her life in New City, Rockland County, on "the dark side of the mountain." Her house was designed and built by her stepfather, the painter and ceramicist, Henry Varnum Poor. Haverstraw, a small industrial town just down the hill from where she lives, has become a recurring subject in her work. "This is my WORK," is how she once described it to a writer.

Poor's Haverstraw is gravel pits, smoke stacks, factory buildings, and power lines. Her painterly response to the grimness of her surroundings is to limit her palette to whites, grays, browns, blues, and pinks. An atmosphere suffused with winter light is conveyed through the application of thin, wash-like layers and delicate gradations of color. Barren yet sensuous, sturdy yet fragile—the artist has found a way to make these aspects of the world an integral part of her painting. The landscape becomes a metaphor for the artist's interior life.

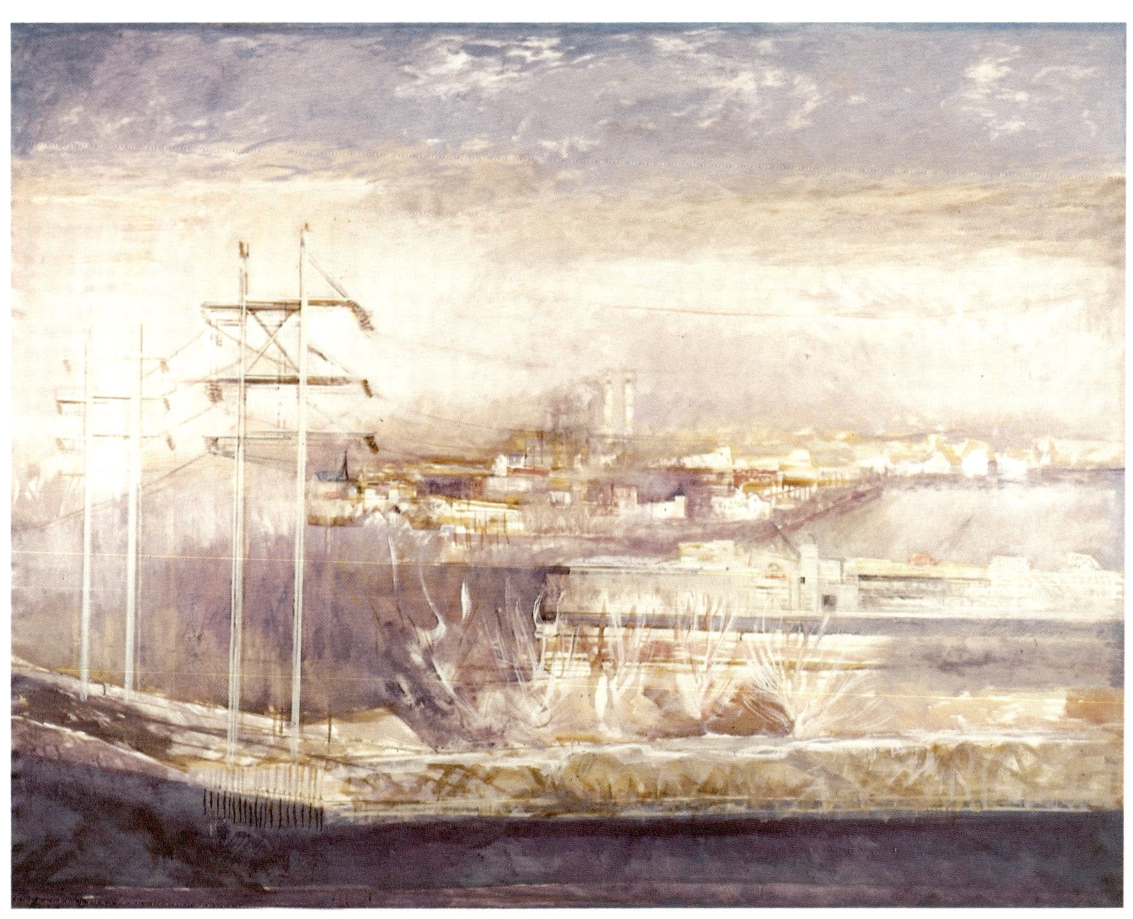

25

Spring Morning on the River
Oil on canvas, 1978
66 x 86 inches
Courtesy Graham Modern

Marjorie Portnow

Alternating her time between Hudson and lower Manhattan, where her studio overlooks the Hudson River and Jersey City, Portnow is a painterly realist who works in formats only slightly larger than those used by Persian miniaturists. Like the miniaturists, she is able to make her paintings into complex visions of the world. Light and atmosphere are transformed into buttery surfaces and evocative color. Both delicate and sturdy, intimate and sensual, the artist's tiny paintings have no trouble holding their own against larger, more obviously dramatic scenes.

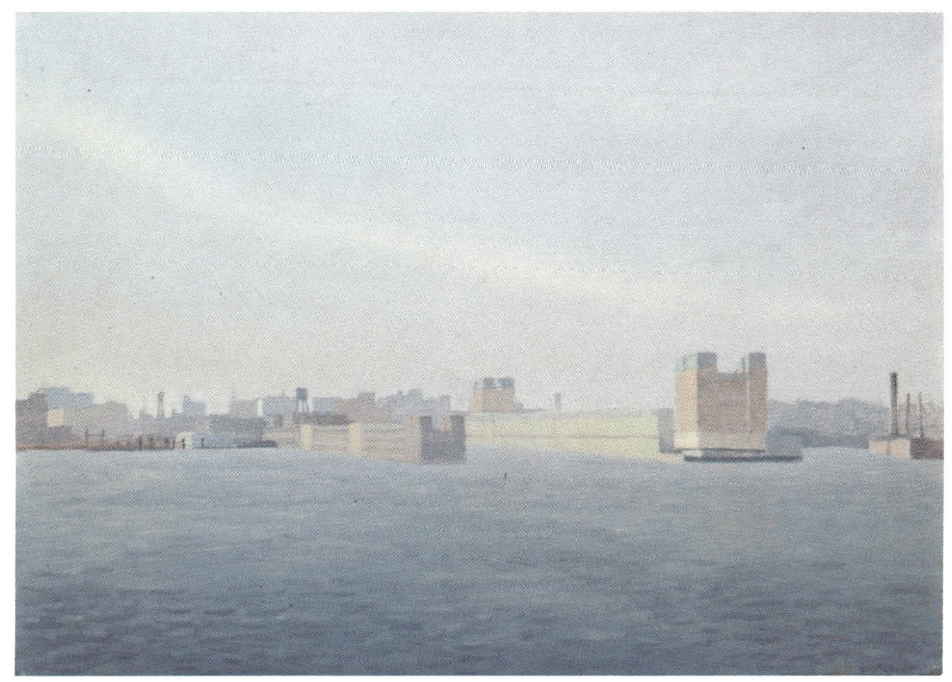

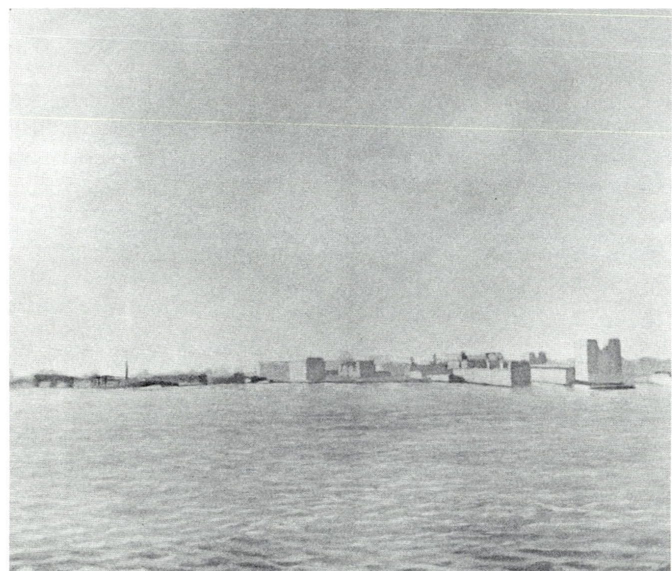

26a   **b**

Across the Hudson on a Grey Day
Oil on canvas, 1978
9¾ x 14 inches
Courtesy Fischback Gallery

View from Vestry
Oil on masonite, 1980
10 x 12 inches
Courtesy Fischback Gallery

The artist is interested in depicting industrial sites and cities from the opposite shore of the Hudson River. In addition, he has painted views from Olana, the home of Frederic Church. Common to all of the compositions are the long view and a delicate, painterly approach. Raleigh's subdued paintings focus on the interaction between atmosphere and place.

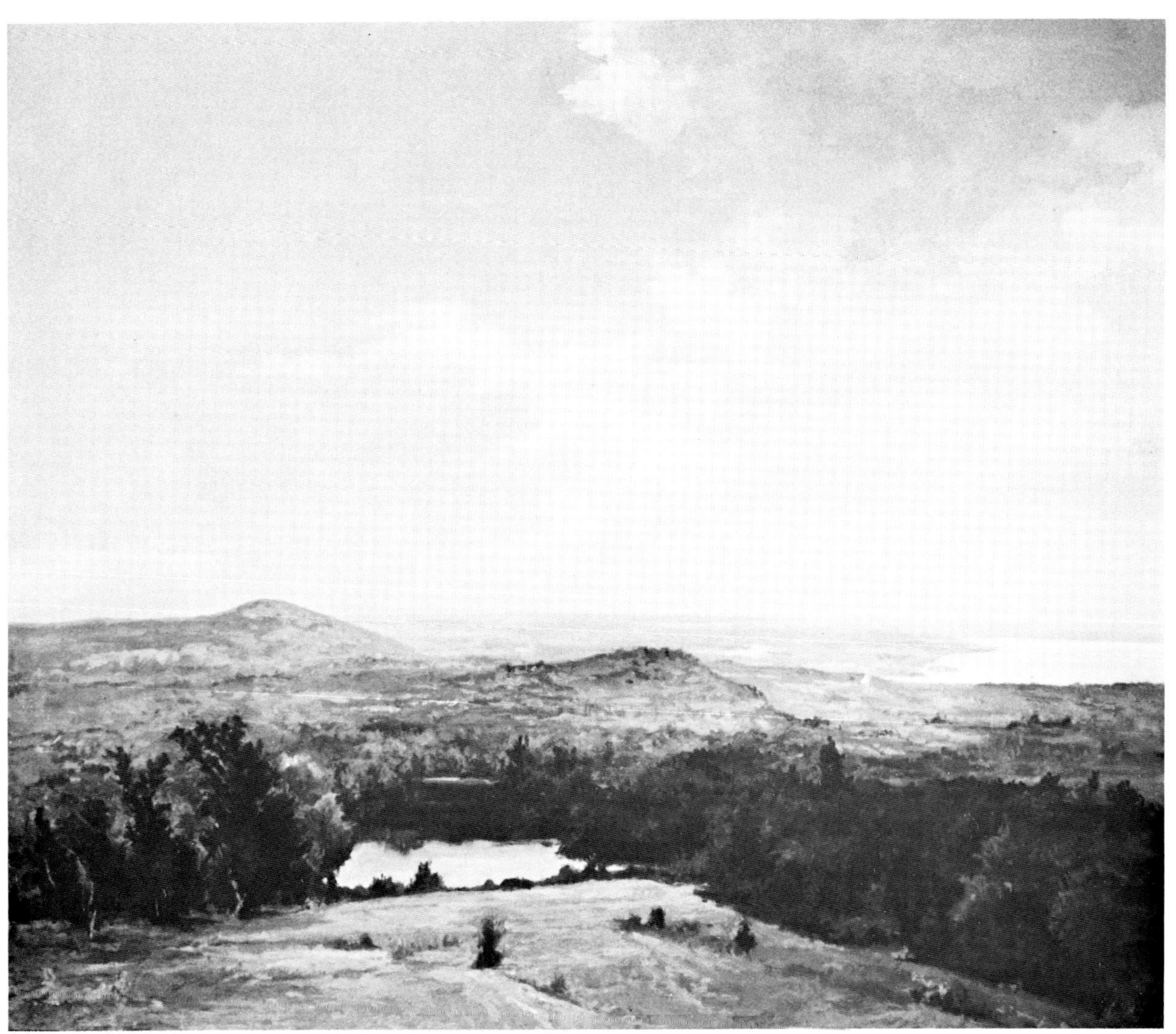

27

Hudson River from Olana
Oil on canvas, 1984
37 x 44 inches
Lent by the Artist

Sylvia Sleigh

The artist became enamored with Bannerman's Island on her first train trip up the Hudson River in 1961. In 1980 she returned to the area with a group of her friends. Her idea was to depict them in front of the ruins that stand on the island. *Invitation to a Voyage: The Hudson River at Fishkill* which consists at this date of 15 panels, forming a 25' x 15' rectangle. Correctly assembled, the painting becomes an imaginative environment blending fact and fiction, realism and fantasy. Deeply knowledgeable in art history, Sleigh synthesized themes and images from Antoine Watteau's paintings with her own ideas about portraiture, human relationships, and social roles.

In her painting of Bannerman's Island, the ruins are depicted as a romantic, sunbathed image. Although the painting is not part of *Invitation to a Voyage: The Hudson River at Fishkill*, it provided the initial inspiration for Sleigh.

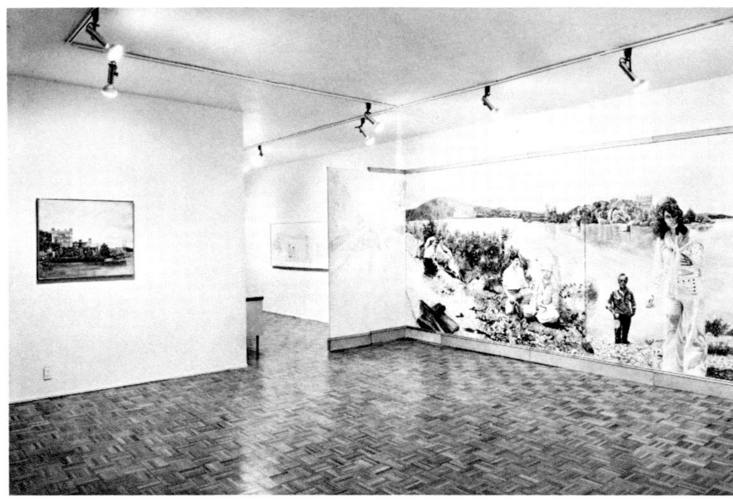

Installation photo of
**Invitation to a Voyage:
The Hudson River at Fishkill**
G.W. Einstein Co., Inc.
January 5 - February 2, 1985

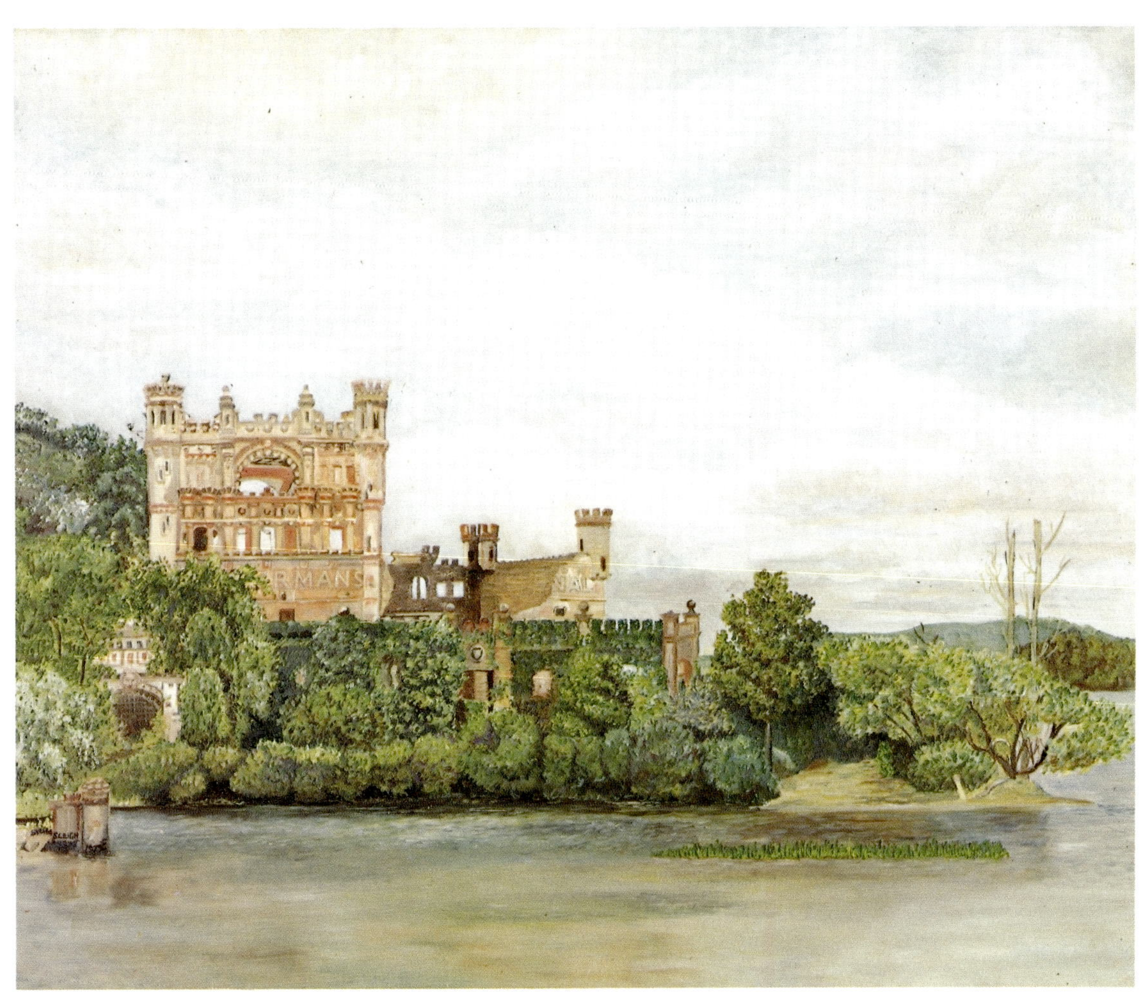

28

Bannerman's Island Arsenal, Fishkill
Oil on canvas, 1979
30 x 36 inches
Courtesy of G.W. Einstein Co., Inc.

The paintings are generous, delicate, sturdy, and bold. They are utopian visions of a fantastic world, but they are neither naive nor syrupy sweet. In terms of his palette, the artist can be seen as an heir to Fauvism, the Viennese School, and the Pre-Raphaelites. The brushwork, however, is busy, expressionistic, and painterly. Densely textured surfaces are crammed with lavish trails and staccato strokes of jazzy color.

Slonem has traveled through South America. His paintings of animals, saints, and vast hordes of Inca gold form separate bodies of work within his oeuvre. Typically, the artist depicts a saint in a tropical paradise complete with birds, animals, and plants. St. Martin de Porres, for example, is shown holding a broom, while Kateri Tekawitha is surrounded by animals common to upstate New York. The world is envisioned as a place that is overripe, fecund, and vulnerable. The artist's empathy is evident everywhere.

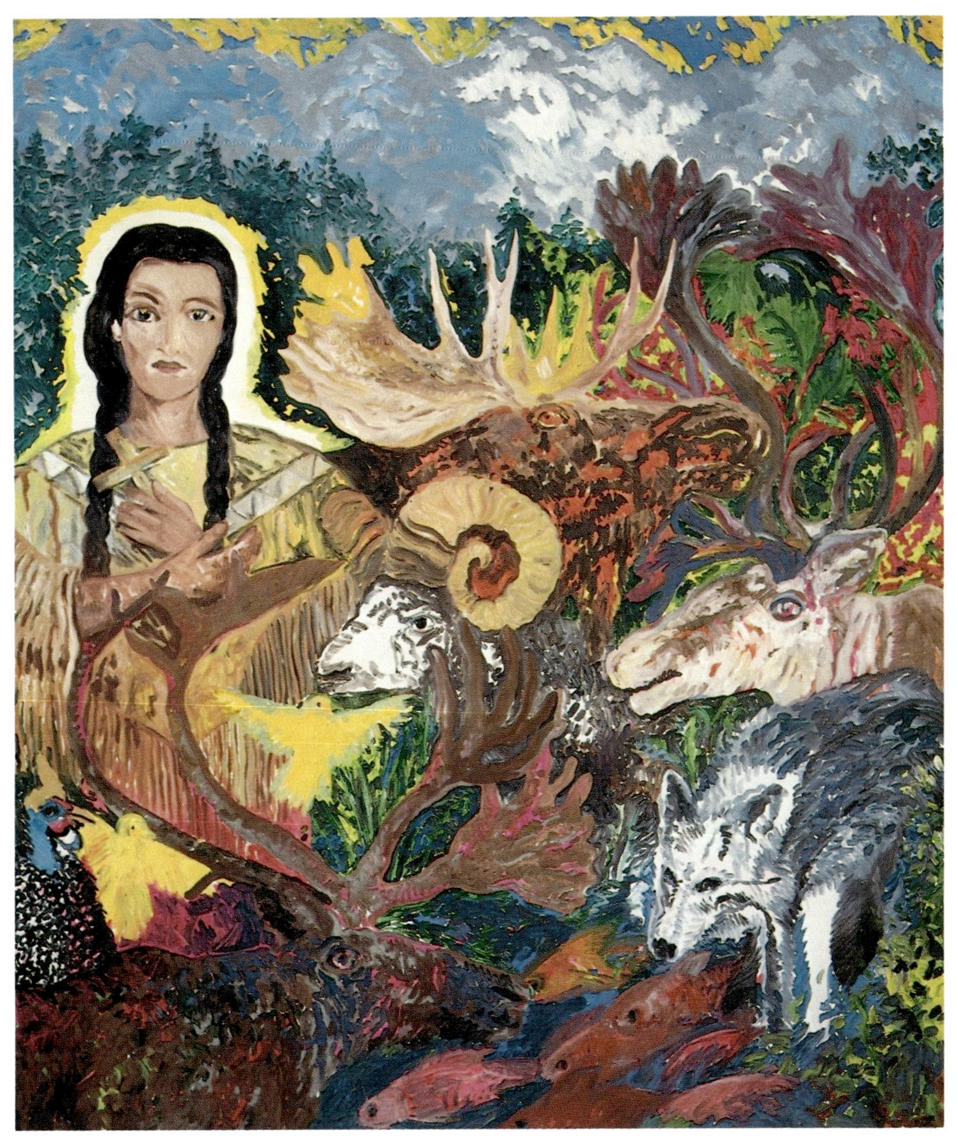

29

Blessed Kateri Tekawitha
Oil on canvas, 1985
72 x 84 inches
Lent by the Artist

Bill Sullivan

The artist regards his paintings as "both symbol and metaphor of some very basic understandings between man and nature, which are almost lost." Since 1965, he has been concentrating exclusively on landscapes, and readily acknowledges his lifelong interest in Frederic Church. Like Church, Sullivan has traveled in South America, in some cases going to the same sites, and painted active volcanoes, lush mountains, tropical forests, impenetrable jungles, lakes, and rivers. He is fascinated by the effects of dawn, sunset, dusk, and twilight—those extreme moments when the mood of a place is defined by the light it is bathed in. His palette is hothouse and theatrical; it is not unusual to find such colors as peach, deep yellow, blood red, pink, and blue in a single painting.

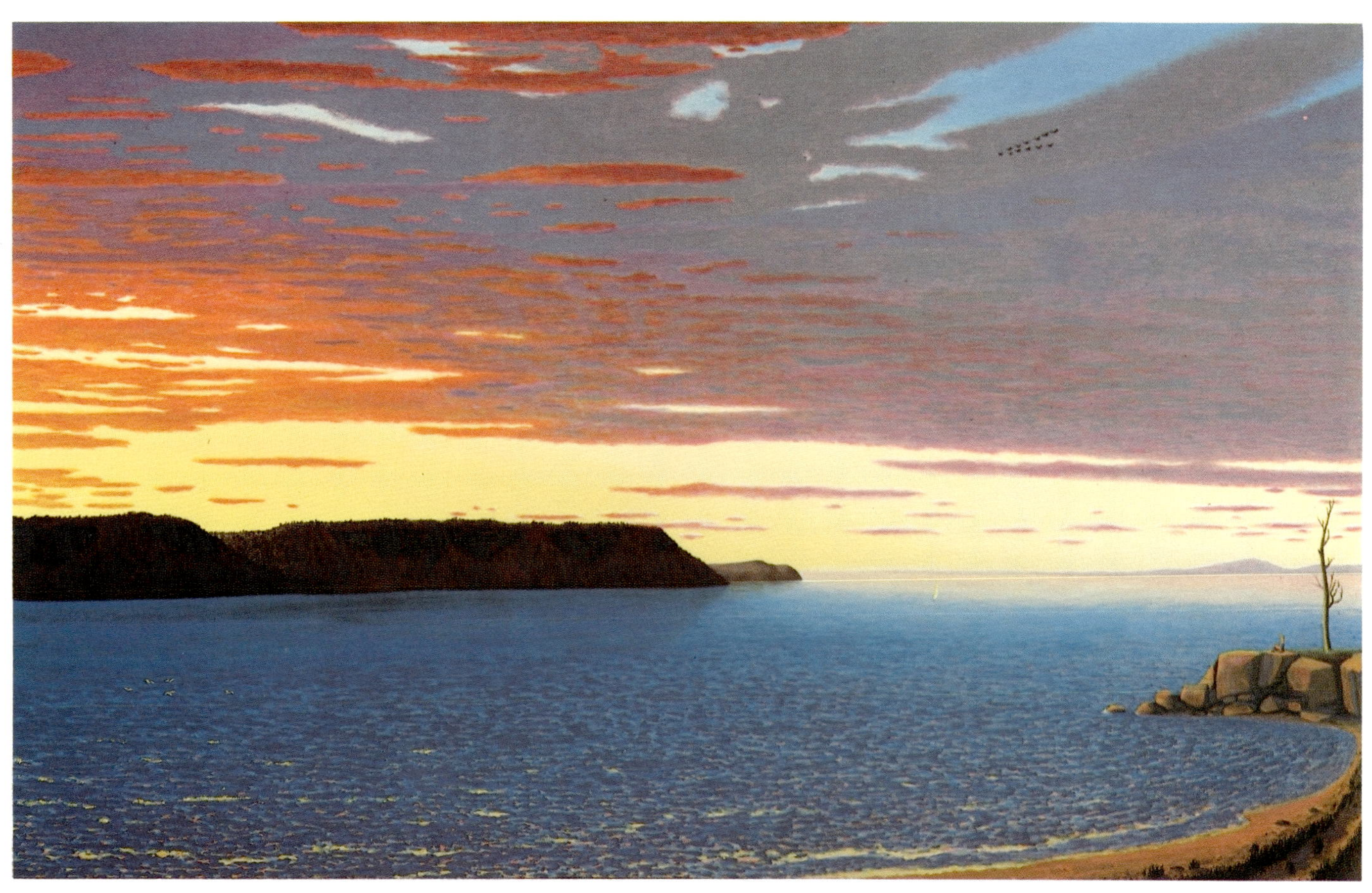

30

Palisades
Oil on canvas, 1984
48 x 78 inches
Courtesy Einstein and Co., Inc.

George Wexler

Shortly after moving to New Paltz in 1957, the artist switched from an Abstract-Expressionist mode to an expressionistic approach to the landscape. By the middle 1960s, he had completely immersed himself in the possibilities of realism. Typically, his paintings are panoramic in scope, while conveying a wide range of details. The paintings tend to be small in scale, their surfaces as smooth as polished teak. The palette is deliberately limited to subtle gradations of blue and green.

For Wexler, landscape is an immense area bathed in light and shadow. He can depict a brightly glowing stand of trees right next to one locked in shadow. A deft master of perspective, he repeatedly documents long views in which farms, factories, roads, bridges, and other signs of man's presence accent or define the landscape. In direct contrast to Frederic Church's painterly exuberance, Wexler approaches his subject matter with a meticulousness that is both respectful and contemplative.

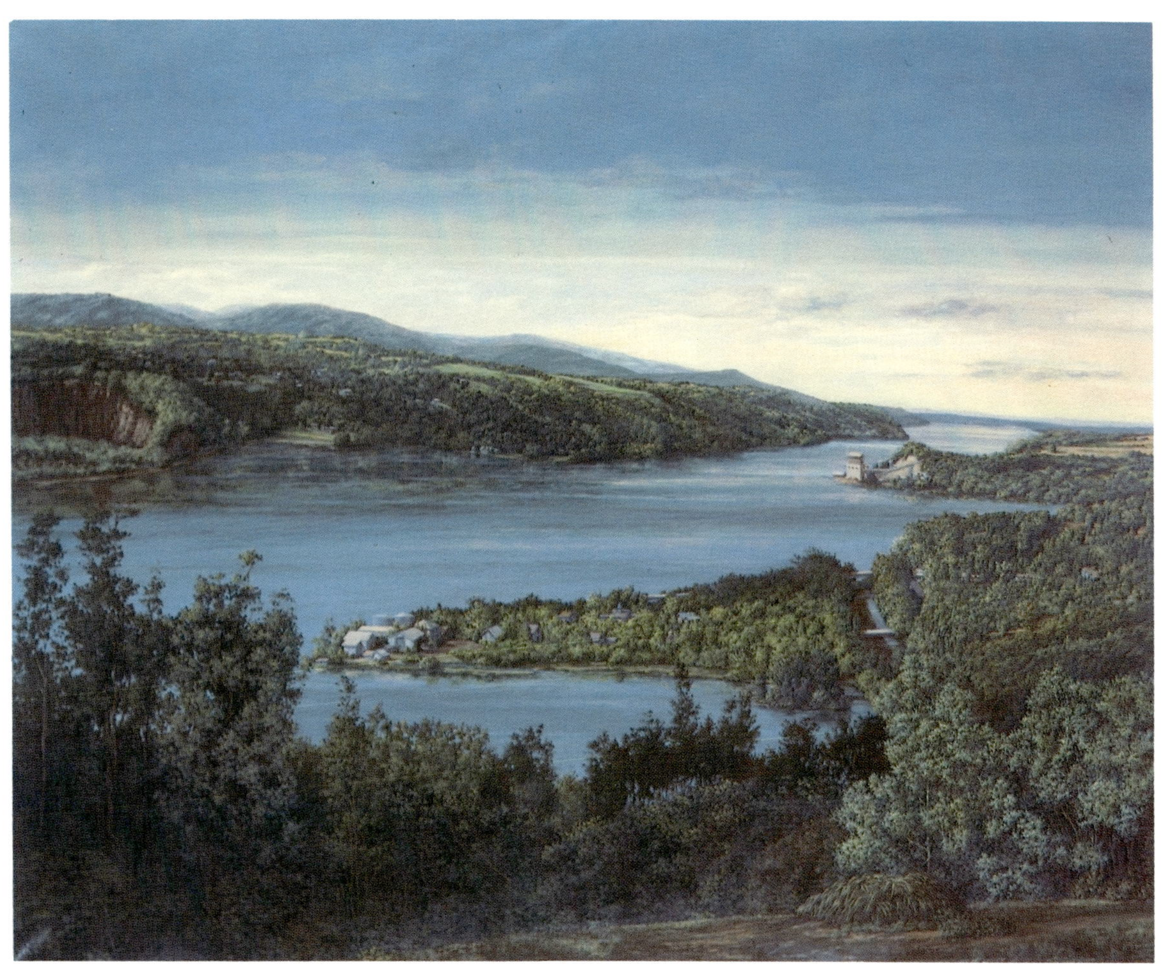

31

Hudson From New Hamburg II
Oil on canvas, 1984
40 x 50 inches
Courtesy Fischback Gallery

William Wilson

The fauna and flora of the Upper Hudson River Valley are only the starting point for William Wilson. Soon his imagination, use of riotous color, and intense, quick brushwork take over and transform his close-up views into a hallucinatory vision in which each plant, leaf, and flower is vividly and vibrantly present. Rather than making a realist counterpart, Wilson uses the visible world as a springboard to reach a dream-like realm where brushstrokes are specific and lyric, controlled and audacious, and color beckons us to leave our habits of seeing behind.

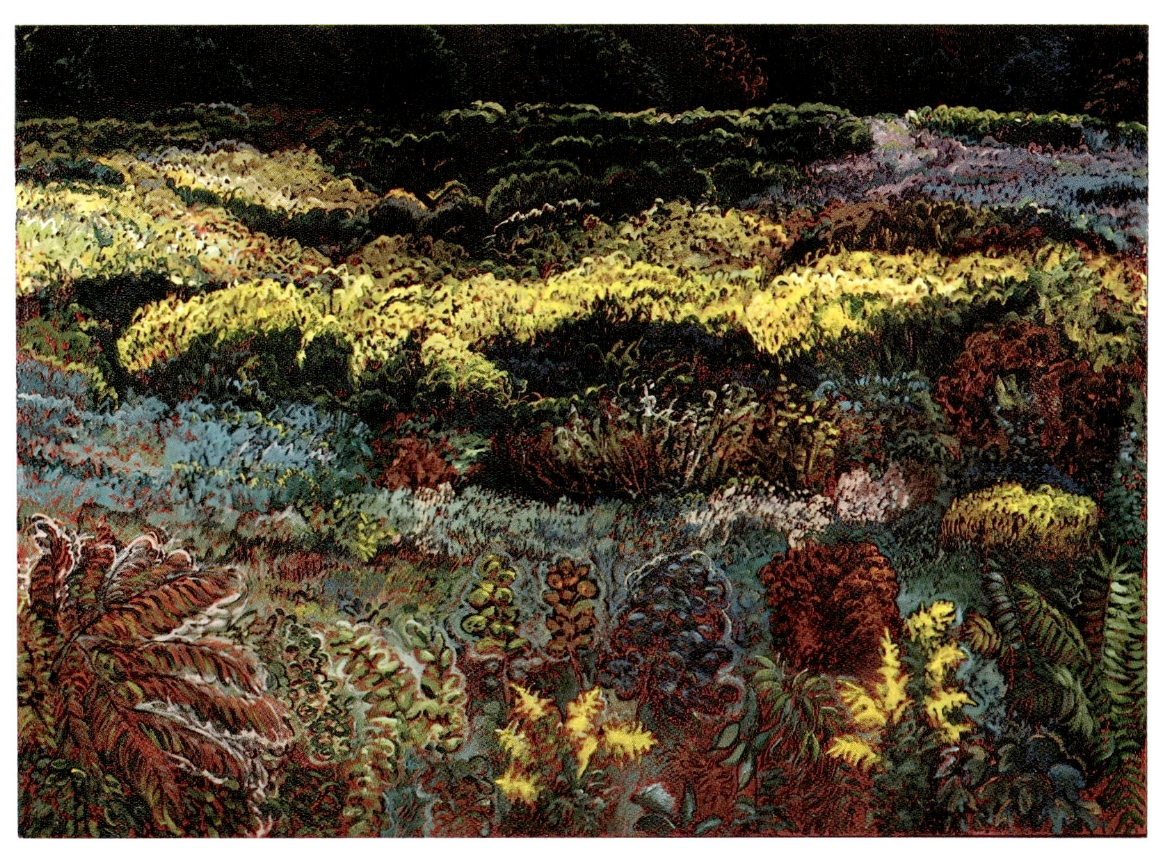

32

Meadow
Oil on canvas, 1985
34 x 47 inches
Lent by the Artist

Albany Institute of History and Art
Claude Bernard Gallery
Ms. Marcia Clark
Ms. Virginia Creighton
G.W. Einstein and Co., Inc.
Equitable Life Assurance Society of the United States
David Findlay Jr., Inc.
Fischback Gallery
Sherry French Gallery
Allan Frumkin Gallery
Graham Modern
Mr. Alan Gussow
Hirschl & Adler Modern
Nancy Hoffman Gallery
Mr. Christopher Jones
Mr. Morton Landowne
Mr. Arnold Levine
Mr. Alex Martin
Mr. Andrew Needle
Mr. Ross Neher
The New Jersey State Museum
Mr. Richard Pitts
Private collection
Mr. Henry Raleigh
Ruth Siegel Ltd.
Mr. Hunt Slonem
Washburn Gallery
Mr. William Wilson